HIDD

HIGHWAYS

OF

NORTH WALES

Ten circular walks exploring Roman roads, drovers' ways, packhorse trails, ancient tracks, and lost lanes - and a ghost story

TEXT & MAPS BY

R J A DUTTON ©1997

PUBLISHED BY

GORDON EMERY
27 Gladstone Road, Chester CH1 4BZ
01244 377955

PRINTED BY

REDWOOD BOOKS
KENNET WAY, TROWBRIDGE, WILTSHIRE BA14 8RN

CREDITS

Thanks to Peter Jones and Steffan John for their help in walking the routes, my wife for companionship, Moira Rae Carter for the cover design, Mike Penney for the photo of the Roman milestone and the Record Office at Hawarden for permission to use it.

As well as publishing, Gordon Emery helped with the text, walked all the routes and allowed me to use excerpts on toll roads from `Guide to the Maelor Way` as well as giving me some information that he had researched on Ogilby`s road through Chirk.

Special thanks to Mr Owen for letting me use the old coach road past his house near Pentrefoelas. One county council had recorded it as public to the county boundary, the other one forgot!

PUBLIC FOOTPATHS

All paths used in these routes are legal rights-of-way unless stated otherwise. Any problems such as missing signposts and obstructions have been reported to the appropriate Highways Authority. Footpaths are the responsibility of the landowner or Highways Authority however the publisher would be happy to forward any letters to the right address with a copy to the Ramblers` Association who try to ensure that the councils carry out their legal duties to keep paths clear.

MAPS

No further maps are needed for these walks but it is advised that you carry an OS Pathfinder if you intend to leave the routes given.

PUBLIC TRANSPORT

Wherever possible, the walks start from bus routes and train stations. Parking details are also given. Walkers should consult up-to-date timetables for leaving and return times before setting out.

CONTENTS

FOREWORD

The author first became interested in Roman roads during the early 1970s having once owned a field with a Roman road across one end of it. With some knowledge of ancient landscapes and construction methods he attended courses on the Roman period and so began to specialise in the search for the most difficult sections of Roman roads.

In 1985 he found most of the course of the Roman road between Chester and Warrington. This took almost five years: a difficult task as the majority of the old road was under the later turnpike. Since then he has found several Roman roads across Cheshire. Having moved to North Wales in the late '80s he has added Roman roads, Roman camps, Saxon sites and moated sites to an ever-growing list.

He hopes you will enjoy these walks and the thrill of walking in the footsteps of our ancestors. If you find other hidden highways he would only be too pleased to know.

Cartoon by the author sent to the publisher whilst looking for a Roman road.

INTRODUCTION

In Celtic times paths criss-crossed the country. Many of the pre-historic routes have survived the plough, and are outlined by the cromlech or standing stones over the hills. Often these old routes were re-used in the Roman network.. The Roman roads in Wales were not as straight as in the lowland countries because there were many more obstacles to overcome but the roads were still reasonably straight. The military roads would usually go over high ground to provide a defensive route from fort to fort, whereas secondary roads were constructed to accommodate wheeled vehicles, messengers and traders between the camps and the settlements.

After the Romans left it was the packhorse trains that kept the Welsh economy alive for over a thousand years. Today, many of these trails are some of the narrow lanes that have been re-used to enable vehicles to reach sheep farms amid the hills. In the lowlands these ancient trails have often been ploughed out leaving only a public right of way. In some of the Welsh villages there are packhorse bridges giving a clue as to where these trains passed through: trains of some twenty to thirty strings of hardy pack animals, each loaded with two wicker baskets fully laden with goods either for market or to sell to the farms along the way. The lead animal had a hoop of copper bells attached which could be heard over a long distance. Travellers would need to stand aside, for these trains would trample anybody in their path.

Since the Norman conquest travellers could find their path blocked by herds of cattle and sheep on their way, perhaps hundreds of miles, to English markets. These animals could be heard coming from afar and farmers would need to lock away their own animals for fear of them getting mixed into the herd. The droves would travel in almost straight lines and quite often very close to the former Roman roads. It was not uncommon for a herd to contain some thirty thousand animals, made up of smaller droves from the outlying hill farms. Many deep rutted scars can still be seen on hillsides where the droves, and the drovers, once passed. In the lowlands many of these routes became cobbled and enclosed between hedges and fences to contain the animals before entering a market town.

The Normans constructed roads between their castles and the large estates. Their construction was very poor in comparison to the Roman roads, more often than not these roads were nothing more than earth tracks. Through the Tudor and Stuart times parishes were responsible for the upkeep of roads within their boundaries. This Highway Act introduced in 1555 remained in force for almost two hundred and eighty years. The Act specified that persons holding land, arable or pasture, with an annual value of £50 or more had to supply two men with oxen, a cart and tools for repairing highways for four consecutive days each year, this was increased to six days in 1563.

Landless cottagers had to work this themselves or find substitutes. Unpaid surveyors were also appointed to inspect highways and bridges and had the right to dig gravel, without paying for it, for road repairs. Unfortunately this act failed and the crude methods of road construction were inadequate to cope with the increase in traffic using the roads in the seventeen century, when wheeled carts were replacing the packhorse, and people were beginning to travel in coaches. Some form of central organisation for construction and repair was needed.

In 1663 the first Turnpike Act arrived and was followed by many others in the eighteenth century. The toll-roads were controlled by Turnpike Trusts who charged a toll at gates or bars along the routes. The improvement of these roads created their own form of genius with new road engineers in the form of: John Metcalf (1717-1810) a blind man who lay stone sets with chippings to fill in the cracks; John Macadam (1756-1836) who used only local stone covered by a graduating smaller stone (he never used tarmacadam as believed); and Thomas Telford (1857-1837) who constructed the London to Holyhead road. Not all the roads were kept in good condition, and not everyone wanted to pay the tolls. Drovers` overland routes avoided the tollgates, and `pikes` were put on top of the gates to prevent horsemen jumping over. In North Wales the 'Rebecca' movement had men disguised as women trying to wreck the gates. These factors helped to bring about the eventual dismantling of the turnpikes so that by the end of the 19th century most roads were repaired by the county councils and the age of the toll roads had virtually ended.

Roads from throughout the ages can be found in North Wales mainly because of the difficulties in farming hills and valleys. The pre-historic tracks can still be found over the hills but in the lowlands many have been ploughed away or re-used in more modern systems. Roman roads can still be found amid the hills although many have had the paving removed and reused in stone walls or for foundations in the Welsh cottages. In the lowlands most are ploughed out or disguised by ditches and hedges criss-crossing them, while some have been reused into the modern system. The scars of the drove roads still remain and some have been surfaced for modern traffic. There are a few remains of the first early coach roads as well and like many of the turnpikes these have been reused in the modern systems.

6

¶ A Proclamation to reſtraine the exceſſiue

Carriages in Wagons, and foure wheeled Carts, to
the deſtruction of High-wayes.

WHere as Wee haue euer had ſpeciall care that the Common high-wayes and Bridges, leading from place to place within this Realme, might be kept in due repaire for the eaſe and good of Our louing Subiects; And obſeruing of late (notwithſtanding the good prouiſion of Our Lawes in that behalfe made, and the conformitie and forwardneſſe of Our Subiects in ſo publique and neceſſary a worke,) That Our high-wayes & Bridges are at this preſent growne into great decay, and very dangerous for paſſage: Wee haue vpon due examination found, That the ſaid decaies are occaſioned by the Common Carriers of this Realme, who for their ſingular, and priuate profite, doe now vſually trauell with Carts and wagons with foure wheeles, drawne with Eight, Nine, or Tenne horſes, or more, and doe commonly therein carry, ſixtie, or ſeuentie hundred weight, at one Burden at one time, which Burden and weight is ſo great, and exceſſiue, as that the very Foundations of Bridges are in many places thereby ſhaken, and the high-wayes and cauſeys furrowed and ploughed vp by the wheeles of the ſaid Carts and wagons, ſo ouerladen, and made ſo deepe, and full of dangerous ſlowes, and holes as neither can Paſſengers trauell thereby in ſafety, nor the Inhabitants or perſons by Law bound to repaire them, be able to vndergoe ſo great a charge. Where, heretofore all common Carriers vſually went with Carts of two wheeles onely, wherewith they could not well carry aboue twentie hundred weight at once, or there abouts, which the Bridges, cauſeys, and ordinary high-wayes did, and might well beare, without any great damage to the ſame.

Wee therefore intending the reformation of the premiſes (and hauing herein taken the aduiſe of Our Iudges, by whom Wee haue bene reſolued, that by the Law of this Our Realme, the ſaid exceſſiue and extraordinary kinde of Carriages. Whereby Our high wayes are thus deſtroyed, are Common Nuſances and Annoyances againſt the weale publique, and an offence againſt Our Crowne) Doe hereby ſtraightly charge, require and command, That no common-Carrier, nor other perſon or perſons whatſoeuer, ſhall hereafter vſe, goe or trauell with any Cart or wagon, made with foure wheeles, to be drawne with aboue fiue horſes at once, alongeſt their Iourney, which will carry in the wintertime as great a weight, and in the Sommer a farre greater Burthen, then the ancient proportion of Carriage was, that the high-wayes and Bridges may hereafter receiue the leſſe damage thereby; vpon paine of incurring Our high diſpleaſure, and to receiue condigne puniſhment, as contemners of our Royall will and Commandement, and to bee further proſecuted and puniſhed for the ſaid Nuſances and Annoiances by fine, and ſuch other wayes, as the Lawes of this Our Realme haue prouided againſt offenders in that kinde.

To which end wee haue expreſly charged, aſwell our Iudges, as our Attourney generall to exact, & require the extremity of Our Lawes in that behalfe: And that euery offender contrary to this Our Proclamation, ſhall for his contempt be brought into Our Court of Starre chamber, there to bee fined and proceeded againſt, according to his demerit. Neuertheleſſe, Our intent, will, and commandement is, and We doe hereby ſtraightly charge, command and prohibit, That no common Carrier whatſoeuer, ſhall by colour hereof take occaſion to inhance, or raiſe the prices of Carriage from any part, or place within our ſaid Realme, vnder paine of our diſpleaſure, and vpon complaint thereof to vs, or our priuie Councell made, to be further puniſhed, as ſhall be thought fit.

And laſtly, we doe hereby will and require all Maiors, Shiriffes, Bailiffes, Iuſtices of Peace, and other Our Officers, and Miniſters in all Counties and priuiledged places whatſoeuer, within this our Realme, That they and euery of them in their ſeuerall Offices, and places doe from time to time prouide, and ſee to the due execution of this Our pleaſure, and Royall Commandement, and that they diſcouer and make knowne all offenders herein, that they may bee ſeuerally puniſhed for their contempts; as alſo that they neglect not, but continue the repayer and maintenance of high-wayes, Bridges, and Cauſeys within this our Realme, according to the Lawes, Statutes and Ordinances now in force, and our Commandement heretofore giuen, as they tender our pleaſure, and will anſwere the contrary at their vttermoſt perill.

Giuen at Our Palace of Weſtminſter the twentieth day of Iuly, in the ſixteenth

Courtesy of Chester Record Office

ROUTE MAP
Not to scale

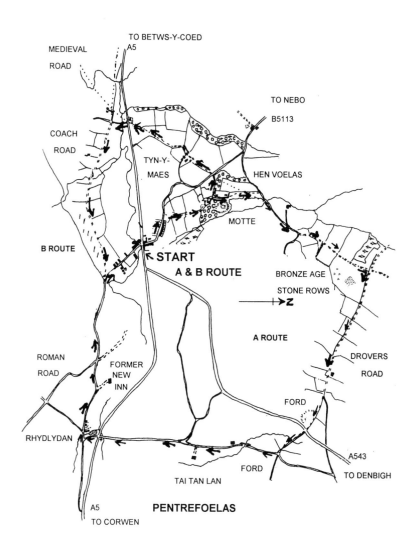

A Drovers`, a Coach Road and More
PENTREFOELAS

START
Village Car Park   SH878513

ROUTE A   6 miles (9 kms)   Ascent 160m
This is a circular walk past a 12th century motte and along a drovers' road, returning to the village by the old London to Holyhead coach road. There are excellent views of rolling landscapes, and the outstanding Snowdonia mountains. There is a cafe, a pub and a shop in the village and another pub serving meals just over halfway around.

ROUTE B   3 miles (5 kms)
The other circular walk passes the century motte and along a different section of the old London to Holyhead coach road, ideal for an evening stroll.

HOW TO GET THERE
By Bus
A bus service is available from Wrexham, Ruthin, Bala and Conwy.
By Car
Pentrefoelas is a small village situated on the A5, on the junction of the B5113 Llanrwst Road   six miles southeast of Betws-y-coed. There is a public car park off the main road by the park opposite the village school.

HISTORY
Several Bronze Age sites lie to the north of the village on the moorland.

The Norman-type motte, slightly north of the present village, at Hen Foelas (old green hill) may have been built by Owain Gwynedd in the early 12th century. All that remains today is the mound which is heavily wooded.

A board by the car park states that Pentrefoelas was an estate village in 1871. Traders and craftsmen worked together making and repairing items villagers used at work or home: everything from socks and shoes to waggons, wheels and ploughs. The old world of rural craftsmen has gone, but the cultural life of the area together with the Welsh language still flourishes.

Setting Out   *From `Coaching Days and Coaching Ways`1903*

DIRECTIONS ROUTE A & B
Leave the car park and go towards the A5. Cross the main road onto the B5113 Llanrwst Road (signposted to Nebo) and walk uphill around the left bend. Go through the kissing gate amid the houses on your right. Take another gate into a field at the rear of the houses. From here turn half-left, and cross to the corner where the field walls meet by another kissing gate. Carry on uphill, along the path which is edged with stones, alongside the wall on your left. Go through the next gate. *Stop for a moment and look immediately to your right where there is a raised outcrop encircled by a ditch. This was a small settlement, which was purposely sited overlooking the valley.*

THE MOTTE

Proceed straight across the field to go through the kissing gate on the edge of a wood. Follow the stony track as it winds its way through the woods. *Was this a chapel site that the track goes around? Yews are normally found in churchyards.* Go into the Hen Foelas farmyard. *Look to your left to see a vaulted icehouse attached to the cottages, and a cross (from the chapel?) built into the wall. Stop for a moment at the farm entrance and by the three-way footpath marker post. On your right there is a man-made mound, built upon a raised earth platform of approximately two acres: this is the motte. When it was first built, there would have been a wooden tower or small wooden castle on the top.*

ROUTE B Turn left. Go to page 15.

ROUTE A

Go half-right and follow the track through the woods. *On your left there is a large rectangular pond. This was a small reservoir for the farm.* Go through the gate ahead, at the perimeter of the woods. Follow the hawthorn hedge on your left, and go through the kissing gate in the far wall, which leads onto a surfaced lane. Turn right, ignore the footpath sign on your left, and continue round the bend and uphill.

When the lane reaches level ground, beyond the cattle grid turn left. Follow a stony track up a steeper section of the hill. After you have gone through the gate at the top of the hill, the track levels out once more. *Look back at the rolling hills with the impressive Snowdonia Mountains like a huge backcloth completing the picture. To your right is a ridge which would have made an ideal defensive position. The mound may be man-made as there are several Bronze Age remains in the area. On the flat field are sets of stones. Three Bronze Age cists with human remains were found here.*

THE DROVERS' ROAD

Carry on through the next field gate. Immediately turn right onto the reed-covered wet road. *This is the remains of a drovers' road used for moving sheep to the midland markets in Cheshire and Shropshire. The road is along the upper side of a wall which was probably constructed by landowners to prevent driven animals straying onto to their land. The wall has been built in a straight line between cultivated pastures and the*

11

Drovers` Road

edge of the moors. There are places along the wall where you will see the original drovers' road higher up the hillside.

Go through three gates and ignore a gated track to your right. A third of the way down the first slope there is a field gate, from here the road is contained between two walls. Continue down the track to where it reaches level ground. Cross the shallow ford. *Stop for a moment; there is another road on your left, which branches off (east northeast) and went to Denbigh market town.*

Resume your walk downhill until the road levels out once more to cross a raised causeway over a marsh area. From here it is but a short walk to a field gate that leads onto the modern A543 Denbigh road. Cross this main road, *to the continuation of the drover's road, which has since been improved and surfaced for vehicles.* The lane descends to a bridge across a stream.

The bridge is the original one. If you look over the fence on the downstream side you will see that it is a clapper type with a flat span. Large stones were placed across stone uprights to provide a platform. The upper surface is the only part of the bridge which has been improved.

Continue uphill, to where the lane reaches level ground and a cattle grid. Beyond this grid there is an old cross lanes. *The lane to your left, which is now fenced across, goes to the old Denbigh Road, which you saw previously. The lane ahead is the continuation of the Drovers' road. The lane to your right, which is improved for vehicles, comes from the south side of the valley.*

THE RETURN

Turn right, along the improved lane, for it is time to make the return to Pentrefoelas. Proceed downhill until you reach the ford. If the water is too deep to walk across there is a small clapper bridge on your right.

Carry on up and over the hill until you reach a road junction. Go half-left and along the lane. *Alongside, the stone walls are built of large boulders.* Eventually go downhill to meet the A5. Cross to the lane opposite and walk to where it meets with another road at the River Merddwr Bridge in the village of Rhydlydan. *This other road was the London to Holyhead coach road, prior to Telford's turnpike.*

LONDON TO HOLYHEAD COACH ROAD

This old major road was in constant use before Thomas Telford constructed his turnpike. A road surveyor was appointed by village leaders, he wasn't paid a salary. It was the duty of every male in a village to take turns in carrying out this task. He was responsible in solving any problems on the coach road, of re-instating worn patches of the track, by getting volunteers from the village to repair the road.

Some villages kept the road in good repair, but in villages where there were only a few residents, the roads suffered. I am surprised that no one has ever written a book about the old coach road. There are many tales to be told about the areas it passed through and the coach stops. One local story has been handed down from father to son about passengers having to alight from a coach and assisting in pushing the coach up a hill. Then, at the top of the hill, the passengers were held up by robbers!

Turn right onto the bridge. *Look over the left parapet, to the two cottages on that side, you will notice that they are not aligned to the bridge. This is because they were built alongside the original road. The first road forded the river on this side. This was improved by the building of a bridge in approximately 1838, after Telford constructed the turnpike. There are no remains of the ford now, the bank has been piled up to create a car space. Beyond the bridge and between the cottages on your left, there is a branch road. This was the continuation of the drove road that you walked downhill to the A5.*

Continue along the road past the Giler Arms Hotel, on your right, to where the lane bends left. *The drive on the your right leads to a cottage originally called the New Inn, a coach stop. The inn has been rebuilt as a modern cottage.* Carry on around the bend and downhill until you come to a small cross roads. *On your left there is an old chapel and village school, both have now gone out of use.*

The crossing road was a Roman road, it ran between Llanfor (Bala) and Kanovium (Conwy). The old ford on the River Merddwr (close to the A5) has been destroyed by the later construction of a mill (Pentre-felin). The Roman road on the north side of the river became the present B5113 Llanrwst Road. In the 18th century the Roman length between Pentrefoelas and Conwy was re-used by the coaches. The mill is now just a private dwelling.

Proceed along the lane past the small farm on your right with a pool and an assorted array of ducks and geese. Continue until you come to the next sharp right bend and branch road on your left. *Stop for a moment and look beyond the field gate ahead and you will see the continuation of the old coach road which today is only a right of way for walkers.*

Carry on around the right bend and pass the modern houses of Pentrefoelas. *Just past Maes yr Afon look for the old, virtually illegible milestone giving 2 miles to Cernioge.* Return to the car park.

14

A Change of Horses   *From `Coaching Days and Coaching Ways `*

ROUTE B

Leaving the farm, the entrance drive goes slightly uphill bending right and then left through an avenue of beech trees, until it terminates on the B5113 Llanrwst Road. *The B road was originally a Roman road which ran between Llanfor (Bala) and Kanovium (Conwy). In the 18th*

15

century the Roman length between Pentrefoelas and Conwy was re-used by coaches. The farm entrance drive was originally a medieval road. It ran between Ysbyty Ifan and the motte.

Cross the Llanrwst road and climb the old stone stile beside the field gate opposite. *In the distance is   Snowdonia which, on a clear day, forms an impressive backcloth to the valley spread out before you.* Stay alongside the wall on your left until you reach a crossing track. Proceed through the gates opposite each other and follow a field access track alongside the wall on your right. *The medieval road originally went through Ty'n-y-maes Farm which is on your left. You will see more remains of this old road lower downhill. The right of way has been re-routed to avoid going through the farm.*

If the next gate is difficult to open, it is quite easy to climb over. Turn half-left and continue downhill keeping a wire fence on your left. When you reach the wall at the bottom of this field, *you are now on the medieval road,* turn half-right and follow the wall/wire-fence on your left. Go through the next field gate and continue downhill beside the sunken track which becomes a stream until you reach the gate at the A5. *Stop for a moment before you go through the gate. The latter part of the track downhill is all that remains of the medieval road. Its continuation on the other side of the modern road, opposite Pont Newydd cottage, has been improved for vehicle access.*

The A5 was a turnpike road, constructed by Thomas Telford between London and Holyhead in the years 1820 and 1828 with a gradient no greater than 1 in 22. Proceed through the gate. **Beware of the traffic** and cross the A5 to the lane opposite the cottage.

Carry on along the narrow lane over the two bridges which span the divided river. *The two bridges were built during the 1830s, one has been rebuilt since.* Carry on uphill until you reach a crossing track. *The medieval road was 200 metres to your right. It continued uphill and eventually connected to an old Roman road, which was the main route between Corwen and Betws-y-coed. A road that was more direct and shorter in distance than either the London coach road or Telford's turnpike.*

16

Turn left and go through the gate, please shut it, and continue along the track. This is not a recorded right-of-way and I am grateful to the owner for permission to use it in this book. Please respect this private land and close all gates. *You will notice that this track is more than just a farm drive, being soundly constructed, thirty-six feet wide and reasonably straight. This was the London to Holyhead coach road prior to Telford's turnpike. Why didn't Telford re-use it? He did, but only in places. He needed to build a road that would be substantially stronger in its design and sounder in its base construction to take the heavier traffic that would use it. He also needed to build bridges, because this older coach road only forded the rivers, and quite often these fording places had unsuitable foundations to support a bridge. Another reason for not using the older road was that it has sunk in several places, and it would be cheaper to make another road, rather than to re-instate the present one. I will point out the sections where it has sunk as you walk.*

Coach Road

When you have gone round the right bend and the track starts to straighten out, look left. There is an earth bank which encloses an area of approximately half an acre, which is now rather wet inside. This was once an animal collecting pound, any animal that strayed onto the road would be put here. The owner of the animals had to pay a fee for their release to the road surveyor. The surveyor was appointed by

17

village leaders, he wasn't paid a salary. It was the duty of every male in a village to take turns in carrying out this task. He was responsible in solving any problems on the coach road, of re-instating worn patches of the track, by getting volunteers from the village to repair the road. Some villages kept the road in good repair, but in villages where there were only a few residents, the roads suffered.

Continue along the road until you are by the access drive to Ty'n-y-Llwyn Farm. *The old road has sunk here. This is indicated by the large amount of modern infill along this section to the next gate.* Look half-left towards the large hill in the centre of the valley. *Where the ruined barn is was a gaer (fort), an enclosed village of the Bronze Age on top of the hill. There are no remains of the enclosure now, it has been ploughed away, only aerial photographs reveal its existence. Situated on the hill top, surrounded by large marshes around the bottom of the hill, was an ideal place to live in those days.*

Proceed through the next gate and follow the road uphill around a left bend to the brow. *On your right there is a large marsh area and in the coaching period this would have been a very dangerous place. Nowadays, with modern drainage, it is almost dry. If you would like to climb the hill to the gaer, now is your chance. There is a footpath (indicated) on you left, which goes over the top of the hill and returns to the village car park.*

For the main route, from the gate follow the old road ahead. *Along this last section you will see more parts of the road that has sunk, caused by collapsed drainage systems under the old surface.* The next gate leads onto the modern road system. *The old coach road has been surfaced and has become part of the modern system through Rhydlydan.*

Turn left and pass the modern houses of Pentrefoelas. *Just past Maes yr Afon look for the old, virtually illegible milestone giving 2 miles to Cernioge.* Return to the car park.

THE END

18

The End of the Journey   *From Coaching Days and Coaching Ways*

ROUTE MAP
Not to scale

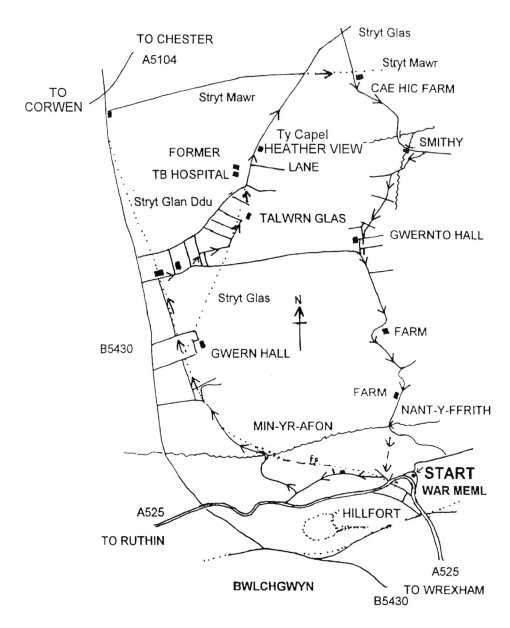

Walking Roman Roads
BWLCHGWYN

START
War Memorial, **A525   SJ263537**

ROUTE 5 miles (8 kms)
The route follows several Roman roads discovered by the author. Other lanes, paths and bridleways have been included to provide you with a circular walk. When you are on or near a Roman road it will say so in the text. Every attempt has been made to clarify where the Roman road came from or goes to. This walk across sheep country is particularly lovely in spring when the fields are full of lambs and the lanes are bordered with daffodils.

HOW TO GET THERE
By Car
Bwlchgwyn is approximately five miles from Wrexham on the A525 Ruthin road. There is parking available by the village War Memorial which is by a sharp bend in the A525.
By Bus
There is a regular bus service to the village from Wrexham.

HISTORY
Bwlchgwyn is a small village situated northwest of Wrexham with a history which goes back into the Celtic period. Sited on a hilltop above the village there is a quarry which has partly destroyed a hillfort, one in a chain of hillforts which guarded the border between England and Wales. The Romans may have used the fort for a watch station over their Ffrith to Ruthin road which passed close by. In the eighteenth and early nineteenth centuries the village was a thriving community from all the mineral quarries working in the area When the ore ran out the quarries closed, leaving a scarred landscape. Today, with many new properties, it is once again a thriving community. The village commands fine views over the Cheshire and Shropshire counties.

DIRECTIONS

Walk west towards Ruthin from the memorial along the main road keeping the valley on the right side. Stay on the pavement until reaching Nant Road on the right. *Opposite is Stryt Maelor, it originally branched from the Roman Ffrith/Ruthin road. Stryt Maelor crossed the main road and is the initial length of the renamed Nant Road. The Stryt was used to transport all the rich ores from the northern Roman quarries to the Roman settlement at Ffrith. It has been traced to Gwernaffield where it branched from another major Roman road.*

Turn right down Nant Road. Ignore the cul-de-sac ahead. The road soon runs parallel to the A525 road above. Pass Pant Glas on the left and a red house on the right. *Stryt Maelor originally passed the red house on the valley side. Just beyond the house is a field gate where the old Stryt went through and onto a terrace which descends the valley side.*

There had been a footpath here but it was closed down and re-routed. Continue with Nant Road to a small cottage on the right. *Note the cottage name: Ty-unos (one night house). It refers to Welsh Common Law which allowed someone to build a house and keep it if there was smoke coming out of the chimney by the next day. There is another example of this is at Betws-y-Coed - namely the Ugly House.*

Continue past the cottage to the hedge on the right where there is a stile. *This is the re-routed footpath which now only leads to the river but is interesting to explore as the remains of the Roman terrace can be seen. The path joins the Roman road and if you only go down to the next stile and look over it, you will see how much an old road becomes overgrown.*

Resume the walk passing Dingle Cottage on the left, and continue uphill to a T junction.

NANT-Y-FFRITH

Turn right and follow the lane downhill passing Brwthyn-y-glyn on the right. Cross the river bridge and follow the lane to the left. *The track on your right by the bridge is the remains of Stryt Maelor which forded the river just below where the river bends.*

Continue with the lane past Min-yr-afon cottage on the right. *The Stryt runs through the cottage garden.* Carry on up the hill. *Look to the right: the Roman road can be seen in the garden running parallel to the lane. In places the old road has been used for a foundation for several shed At the top of the hill the Stryt combines with the lane.* Walk along the lane past Ty-gwyn Farm on the right until reaching a sharp bend left.

GWERN HALL
At the sharp left bend there is a field gate across a stone track. To the right of the gate there is a wooden railed stile. Follow the stone track until it bends right and then along the footpath straight on into the field, keeping close to a stone and earth embankment on the left once through the field gate. *You are now on the Roman road.*

On the approach to the stile set in an estate wall. *The camber of the old road can be clearly seen before it passed under the wall In the estate the footpath is in the Roman ditch and the road can be seen to the right of the trees that line the verge. The road is intact and the full width, ditch to ditch, is ten metres.* Leave the avenue of trees and enter into the field to the front of Hall.

The Hall was built as a wedding present and it has the appearance of a monastic building. It commands a fine view of the Llandegla Moors to the west. In the front field there has been a lot of ground disturbance. This is due to the removal of a branch Roman road known as Stryt Glas (Green Street) and you will see this again later.

Continue across the field and go through two field gates opposite each other. Turn right, and almost immediately, turn left at the trees. *Once again the path is in the Roman ditch and the road can be seen in the trees.* Leaving the wooded area the path follows the field boundary bank. *There is no evidence of the road across this part of the fields.*

The next stile is set in the wall. *The Roman road (Stryt-Glan-ddu) passed through the farm opposite the stile on its way to Rhydtalog.*

Turn right along this lane passing a red brick bungalow on the left. Look for the first field gate (black metal) on the left, close to the bend in the lane. This is a bridleway. Follow the tractor ruts over the field which turns to the right and then through a gate and straight on until reaching a bend to the left. *Stop and look to the right and the rise of the slight hill. A hollow runs down the slope to be parallel with the right fence of the bridleway. This is Stryt Glas mentioned earlier at Gwern Hall. The road originally was a connection to the Ffrith/Caerwys Roman road from Bwlchgwyn.*

The bridleway continues past the ruins of Talwrn Glas Farm on the right. Just beyond the ruins look for two tall stone gate posts on the left. Turn left by the second and go diagonally across the field between two reed hollows. *Here you will notice a track on the left. This is the remains of Stryt Glas.*

Stryt Glas

Carry on across the field to the far corner where there is a bridlegate. *The old road now becomes more evident although very overgrown with brambles.* There is a clear path through created by horse riders. Once clear of the briars the road width is cleared of vegetation by farm vehicles.

The large wooden buildings on the left were once a TB Hospital for the poor before the last World War. They are now used for outward bound pursuits for children from Manchester and Liverpool.

The bridleway becomes a surfaced road. Ignore the lane to the right. *Look for Heather View on the right. This had been a chapel and is now converted to a normal dwelling house.*

Stryt Mawr

25

STRYT MAWR

Continue straight along the lane until reaching another lane on the left. *This lane had been a Roman military road between Chester and Brithdir (Dolgellau), and in a later period re-used with part of Stryt Glas for the Chester to Bala coaches.*

Originally there was a cross roads here. Opposite the left lane there is a bridleway where you should turn right and follow its track. *Through the bridlegate the width of the Roman road can be seen. In this wilderness it is even more outstanding.* Continue when the old road narrows. *This part of the road has been taken into the boundary of a poultry farm.* The bridleway exits onto a modern lane by Cae Hic Farm. *The Roman road once passed to the left side of the farm on its way to Coed Talon.* Turn right along this lane..

CAE HIC FARM

The farm was built in the 17th century, but one of the buildings to the rear of the farmhouse is from the 13th century. It had been a chapel alongside the reused Roman road and it still contains one of the original chapel windows.

Carry on along the lane. *Those of you with sharp eyes will notice implants of holly opposite each other in the side hedges. These indicate old tracks before the construction of the lane.*

SMITHY COTTAGE

Follow the lane downhill and over the narrow bridge. Ignore the footbridge on your right which takes a footpath to the chapel seen earlier. Go up and over the small bank. Go past the white cottage. *This was a smithy, hence its name. The bellows were driven by a water wheel which was in the centre of the building. The cottage was built astride the stream which still runs beneath it today.*

Take the sharp right turn onto a bridleway, pass over a small bridge and turn left before the stone gateposts onto another bridleway. *This was an estate drive which ran between Ffrith Hall in Nant-y-Ffrith and Pentre near Treuddyn. Ignore the next bridleway on your right.*

26

GWERNTO HALL

The hall stands empty of human occupation. The lower rooms have been used for pigs. The walled garden is a wilderness. The wall is soundly constructed and its original entrance gate is still in place. Follow the wall until its return into a farmyard.

Do not go into the farmyard but take the bridlegate ahead and follow the hedge on the right. *Look over this hedge and the continuation of the old estate drive can be seen to be blocked off by a stone wall.*

Look for the bridlegate along the right hedge which will bring you onto the south entrance of the hall. Turn left along the lane and continue through an avenue of tall beech trees. Follow the lane for a mile as it winds its way past a farm on the left. *The old estate drive originally went to the left of the farm.*

You should go up the hill and round a bend, downhill and over a cattle grid until you reach a sharp left bend. *The estate drive continued as the lane until reaching a cottage then turned right into Nant-y-Ffrith valley. The Hall was demolished at the turn of the century and the site was planted over by the Forestry Commission. Look at the OS map or explore the area to find several pleasant walks in this valley.*

Turn right at this bend and continue down the lane over a small bridge, then follow the lane through a farm. Dig in your heels and go down the steep hill to the Nant-y-Ffrith bridge. As the lane bends left from the bridge, take the footpath stile in the right corner. Follow the overhead wires up the hill. *Those of you who prefer an easier way to the top of the valley can follow the lane to the left which will eventually come to a T junction. Turn right and the lane will come to the village memorial: approximately 3/4 mile.*

As the footpath climbs the hill it goes across two tracks, the first was a quarry road and the second one is much older. This was the access road to the farm which you just passed through. At the stile turn left and walk up to Nant Road. Turn left and continue to the main road above, turn left again and back to the village memorial.

THE END

27

ROUTE MAP
Not to scale

MEADOW VIEW

GOLDEN GROVE INN

BURTON LANE

HONKLEY FARM

OLD SCHOOL

TOWN DITCH

B ROUTE

N

SHORDLEY HALL

RACKERY FARM

B5373

RACKERY HALL

SILVERDALE

B5373

GWASTED FARM

BRYN-Y-GAER

A541 TO WREXHAM

A550

RIVER ALYN

CASTLE

CAERGWRLE

CAR PARK

A541

START

TO MOLD

A & B ROUTES

An Ancient Packhorse Trail
CAERGWRLE

START
Public car park, High Street SJ305575

ROUTE A 9 miles (14 kms)
The longer route passes the Golden Grove Inn halfway round. Parts of the route are muddy but a road diversion to the worst part is given.

ROUTE B 6 miles (10 kms)
Parts of the route are muddy but a road diversion to the worst part is given.

HOW TO GET THERE
By Train
Caergwrle is on the Wrexham/Bidston line. From the station, walk down the hill and fork left up Castle Street to the village.
By Car
The village lies approximately halfway between Wrexham and Mold on the A525. The public car park is alongside the village main street.
By Bus
A bus service is available between Wrexham and Mold through the day.

HISTORY
For over a thousand years the Welsh economy was kept alive by the packhorse trains. Travelling in strings of some twenty to thirty animals, usually in the care of two drivers, these animals were specially bred for their surefootedness through the Welsh hills. They travelled with large baskets hung either side of each animal. The leaders carried half hoops of copper bells strapped across their backs; these acted as a warning to other travellers of their approach.

The trails made by these trains negotiated into areas where no wheeled vehicle could go, passing through some of the wildest and the best

29

beauty spots in Wales. The wear and tear on the trails was tremendous, many became water causeways for mountain streams, causing the trains to move over and cutting another trail. In 1691 an Act was passed by the Government of the time 'that no horse-causeway to be less than three feet wide'. Bridges were built over dangerous rivers while several fords were cobbled across shallow streams.

Many of these trails can still be found today, either as waterways or footpaths, some have been incorporated into the narrow Welsh lanes, and bridges still span the rivers. One of the busiest trails which can be found in places is the Chester to Corwen trail. Over one hundred trains a day would use this trail entering Wales. Although ravaged by the plough in several places, parts of the trail still contain the old right of way and it is outlined by public footpaths and bridleways.

The Chester/Corwen trail went through Dodleston, Caergwrle, Ffrith, and Bwlchgwyn. In the Llandegla Vale two trails branched off to the northwest. The main trail continued along the foothills of the Llantysilio Mountains into the Vale of Corwen, where it once again, divides into several branches.

I have chosen to take you along an interesting part of the trail which lies between Caergwrle and Dodleston, returning on another old trail that was a major drovers` road which passed close to Caergwrle, and came from the Vale of Clwyd. In the 17th century roads were poor and the wet marshes of Burton were an obstacle to travellers. Iron, and possibly coal, was transported to Chester from Ffrwd where, in 1699 Edward Lloyd mentions coal mining at Windy Hill. `Whimseys`, worked by horses in pairs for two hour shifts wound coal up the shaft. The ironworks paid to surface `Cobblers Lane` and the causeway across the marshes.

DIRECTIONS

From the car park cross the High Street. (There are pedestrian lights to your left.) Turn right to reach the Spar shop opposite the Post Office. Turn left along Castle Street and take the left fork in the road. Turn left along Derby Road as far as the Derby Arms. *This inn was originally thatched.* Turn right into the narrow walk-way beyond the inn which goes quite steeply downhill to the River Alyn and the packhorse bridge.

30

PONT-Y-DELYN

The bridge, once recorded as Pont-y-Dorlan, is a long narrow structure for it crossed the main river and an ancillary arm which once fed a water driven sawmill that was close by on the east bank. The track-way of the bridge has been raised to accommodate a gas main under the parapet. The dating of the bridge is difficult matter as there were no records kept. It is probably one of the oldest bridges over the River Alyn and is the best example of this type of bridge in North Wales. It is assumed to be of the late 17th century and it is a picturesque and historical survivor of an age gone by. Nowadays this bridge is used constantly by the local inhabitants perambulating between Hope and Caergwrle.

Pont-y-delyn

Cross the bridge and walk up Fellows Lane which has a mixture of old and new properties. Go over the railway bridge of the Wrexham/Bidston line and continue along the lane until it reaches the Wrexham/Hawarden main road. Beware of the traffic. On the opposite side there is a concrete drive to Rhyddyn Farm. *The farm deeds date from 1697.* Go over the stile, halfway up on the right, and turn left along the path which climbs uphill to another stile. *You are now on Wat's Dyke which is outlined by the row of trees on the north side of the farm. It has been destroyed directly behind the farm.*

From here keep straight on avoiding the spreading brambles. Once clear of the brambles the route of the path runs alongside a wall, which borders the wooded hill of Bryn-y-gaer. **Buried deep under the grassy surface are the cobble stones of the road which is three metres wide. These cobbles were laid in the 17th century to re-instate the trail that was showing considerable wear and tear from the continual strings of packhorses. Further up the hill the cobbles have all been removed.**

From the highest point of the footpath the village of Hope can be seen to the northwest and the village church where Saxon stones and millstones can be found built within the church walls. Bryn-y-Gaer, on your right, translates as hill of the fort. In the trees and encircling the top is the remains of a Bronze Age hillfort, which has been half destroyed by a stone quarry. In the 1920s Bryn-y-gaer was quite bare of trees.

CAER ESTYN

Continue along the path keeping the wooded hill on your right. At the far end of Bryn-y-gaer the hill slopes down quite quickly to field level. The entrance to the quarry, now being used as a landfill site, can be seen on the right. Go over the stile by the entrance gates and turn left to the main. Llay/Hawarden road (B5373). *This was once a main Roman road which ran between Whitchurch, Tallarn Green. Isycoed, Gresford, Hope, Padeswood, Mynydd Isa, and Northop.*

Turn right along the main road for ten metres and take the stile in the hedge opposite. Turn half-right and go down the sloping field to climb a stone stile, then continue in the same direction to a gate and stile on the corner of the Gwern Estyn Lane. The footpath now keeps the hedge and buildings on your right. *Notice the old trail going to your left. This was the packhorse route and it goes around the hill to the meadow below. It runs alongside the hedge on your left and goes through where your next stile is.*

Watering the Horses

Descend into the lower meadow and go to the far corner where there is a hidden stile. Turn left, go through the gate and along the entrance drive to Silverdale Cottage. (Ignore the dog, just go slowly, her bark is worse than her bite.) *Silverdale can be traced back to the 16th century. It was a watering pool for packhorses on their way to Chester. The pool or pools are mentioned in early church records as receiving a blessing from travelling monks. No records can be found as to whether the trains had to pay for the privilege of watering their animals here.*

Go straight on through the field gate and another across the field. Turn half-right keeping a mature hedge on your right. *Notice again the old road alongside the hedge being re-used for a waterway.*

SHORDLEY HALL
Where the ditch curves away to the right, head across the fields to Shordley Hall and Shordley Lane. *This is almost the original route of the trail. Originally it went straight across the lane from this last stile and kept Shordley Hall on the left. The right of way has been re-routed and we shall see the old trail later.*

Turn right along the lane until the road bends slightly right. From the stile on your left the path runs ahead alongside the old course of the brook. *The brook on your left is from a later period.* At the next hedge take the double stile. Turn half-left across the field and go through the fieldgate by the scrub and trees. Keep the hedge on your left. *This is where the packhorse trail came through. When the field is ploughed this part is littered with cobbles.*

ROUTE A   Go on two paragraphs.

ROUTE B
Continue to the hedge directly ahead and stop. *Look into the next field and you will see the impression of the old trail going directly to the front of Oaktree Farm. See next page for details of Town Ditch and the corpse road.*

CORPSE ROAD
Turn right keeping the hedge on your left. At the next corner go down the bank of the ditch and onto a scatter of stones. *These are the remains of an*

old ford. Over the stile continue with the hedge on your left, then beyond the next bridge and stile keep the hedge on your right until you reach an oak tree at the next corner. Now continue straight across to a field gate that can be seen in the far hedge. Go through the gate onto the lane and turn right. ***You are now on a drovers' road.***

Proceed as page 40.

ROUTE A continued
Go over the small bridge and stile on the left near the next field hedge. Turn right and go to the corner of the field hedges. ***Directly ahead, you can see the impression of the old trail crossing the next field towards the front of the Oak Tree farmhouse.*** Follow the hedge to the stile opposite the building on the Town Ditch Lane.

TOWN DITCH
Town Ditch was the name of a Saxon village. The defence camp, a raised earth platform protected by a ditch and dyke, a common Saxon practice, still has 90 metres of ditch remaining in the grounds of the Manor House, on your left. The present building dates to the 16th century. Its decorative Tudor chimneys were removed this century. The wooded area to the rear of Oak Tree Farm on the right was the main village. In 1988 I found a Saxon mill which was on the brook that runs to the rear of the woods. The mill pool has since been filled in, only the platform of a wooden building remains.

CORPSE ROAD
The hedge that you walked along to the stile on Town Ditch Lane was originally an old road. There is a public footpath along this hedge to the south which exits onto Cobblers Lane, where we will meet it later. The old road can be found only in places where the plough cannot reach. It was traced through in 1989 and it was found to run between the Gresford Church and the Hawarden Church on a very straight line.

The width of the road was only one metre wide. It was made of small cobbles neatly placed together and an edge kerb which kept the cobbles from spreading. The name is rather bizarre, being known as a corpse road.

In many parts of the country, particularly in the more remote areas, the establishment of the churches did not keep pace with the growth of the population. Thus enormous parishes survived, and although there were subsidiary chapels in these large parishes, only the parish church had the right of burial. Consequently the dead had to be carried there to be buried. The large number of deaths by the plague in 1348-9 hastened the creation of new parishes.

BURTON

Turn right along the lane between the Manor House and Oak Tree Farm for approximately two hundred metres. A footpath sign can be seen on the left. *The present lane which continues to bend to the right goes to Golly. Originally the road did not bend where it does today, but continued straight on across the fields to Burton Green. On the brook lower down the fields a small bridge remains as a reminder of the old road. The road although ploughed out, still contains the right of way and is just a footpath across the fields today.*

There are two paths from the lane, the left branch is a re-route, it originally was the main packhorse trail through Honkley Hall. The trains then passed through Dodleston close to the motte (Norman fort) and continued on the route of the present lane to Balderton. They would have crossed the Balderton Gutter by way of the old Roman ford, which is slightly upstream of the present road bridge continuing their journey to Chester on the present Lache lane: now you know why the lane bends so much. The Roman road ran slightly to the northeast of the lane, on higher ground. The trains would not use the Roman roads due to the road stones wearing away their small light shoes. The path which goes straight on and down the fields was the Caergwrle toolmakers` trail to Chester Market which you are now going to follow as the Honkley Hall route is no longer a public right of way.

HONKLEY FARM

Go straight across the first field to the stile and continue through the second field and through the gate ahead (not the one on your right). *The toolmakers` trail originally took more of a straight line to Honkley Farm from the lower half of the second field.*

Continue across the third field and go through the field gate. Turn half-right to use another field gate by a water trough. The path then continues in the same direction across the next field through the gateway, keeping buildings to your left. Continue through the farmyard gate and go between the barns onto Stringers Lane. *The trail originally went to the right of the farm; the farmhouse has been built on it.*

Turn right along Stringers Lane and look for the stile opposite the farmhouse *The name `Stringers` comes from the packhorse days. It refers to the strings of packhorses which travelled along it calling at farms between Hawarden and Rossett.*

Go over this stile. The footpath keeps the hedge on your right. From the next stile go straight on. *Directly in front of you can be seen the very wide stretch of Burton Marshes. In 1994 I saw these meadows flooded even though it is now a well-drained area. Soon we shall be coming to the only way across even when it is flooded.*

In the lower half of the second field the hedge starts to curve to the right and the stile becomes obvious directly ahead of you. From here go directly ahead to the gap in the far corner of the field. Turn left and go along the lane past Meadow Farm. Cross the wooden bridge.

DODLESTON
Stop for a moment. Directly in front of you is a raised causeway to Dodleston constructed in the 17th century by the Ffrwd Ironworks. When the marshes flooded this causeway remained quite dry. It has been used by many travellers as well as the Caergwrle toolmakers. Although the causeway was constructed before the tool road to Chester it may still have been in use afterwards. There are records of packhorse trains avoiding the tollgates because of their ability to travel over most types of terrain. One of these tollgates was further downstream at the Pulford crossing.

Obviously the causeway has had more layers added to it for the movement of farm vehicles, but since the meadows have been well drained the causeway is little used and has become very overgrown with grass. From this bridge to the far side of the meadows is still a public bridleway but unfortunately both access routes to the bridleway are either footpaths or

37

private driveways. How this strange anomally came about cannot be ascertained but it is likely that the parish council in Burton thought that the driveway was a public road, whilst at the far side of the marshes the parish council in Cheshire may have made a similar mistake. To get onto the bridleway by horse or bicycle you now need the owner's consent.

Golden Grove Inn

GOLDEN GROVE INN

Immediately turn right and walk along the field with the ditch on your right. The footpath goes across the first field and over the stile by the gate. Continue along the edge of the ditch then turn right across the bridge and follow the tractor road across the field. The stile is to the right of the field gate on the Burton Green lane. Turn left along the lane for fifty metres to the Golden Grove Inn on the right. *Despite claims to be a 12th century coaching inn (coaches did not even run to Chester until the 18th century) the inn dates to the 16th century and it was a drovers' stop. When the owners purchased the inn and started interior renovations they found the indications of iron rings which had been*

38

inserted into the walls at regular distances around the rooms. These rings came from the drove period.

A leather strap would be inserted through the rings, and any drover who wanted to stay the night, for the cost of half a penny, used this method: the man would stand against the wall, draping his arms over the strap, and then would slump down to sleep and hang there overnight. If you could afford to spend a penny, then you could sleep on straw laid on the floor. At the rear of the inn a large compound was found. This was probably where the animals were kept overnight.

The drovers would continue their journey to Chester by the Pulford crossing. For here there is a field called 'Moot Field'. Moot means meeting place and this may have been the medieval version of a car boot sale. On a moot field stalls would be set out and a lot of trading took place. These fields can only be found at major cross roads or fords where busy roads meet.

The drovers would continue to Chester over land which is now owned by the Westminster Estate. Sections of the old road can still be found but these are only used today for field access.

THE RETURN
Leaving the inn go back the way you came toward the last stile, but continue along the lane as it winds its way to Burton Green. *The ditches either side have been inserted since the lane became surfaced for motor vehicles, probably in 1890. Prior to this there were no ditches and no hedges.*

Follow the lane passing Burton Hall lane on the left and Stringers' Lane on the right and continue into the small hamlet of Burton Green. *On the right, and at the end of some recently built houses, there is a two-storey cottage which is from an earlier date than the houses. There is a footpath finger post tucked into a corner between the cottage and the field. This path is the termination of the old Town Ditch road which I mentioned earlier.*

Continue along the lane which now bends slightly left and right passing the cottages on the left. Go past the Burton village lane on the left. *The next building on the left is the converted village school to a normal dwelling.*

The lane from here narrows and this is because part of the right side has been incorporated into farm land. The main reason for this is due to later travellers avoiding a wet stretch of the track. When the Land Enclosure Acts came into force a lot of these avoidable stretches were enclosed into field systems. A slight bend in the present lane was created.

Continue along the lane past the Golly lane on the right and onto a long straight section which now starts to go uphill. *On the OS maps this section of the lane is called 'Cobblers Lane'. On Tithe maps it is called 'The Lane of Cobbles' and under the tarred surface that is exactly what is there - cobbles. Constructed this way by the Ffrwd Ironworks in the 17th century when horses pulled heavy carts, the cobbles gave the animals a much better grip on the surface than loose stones.*

On the right is St Michael's Cottage. It has nothing to do with saints. Have you ever been to Marks and Spencer`s store in Chester? One of their managers once lived here. Look over the hedge opposite the cottage and notice the very long dried-out hollows. These were drinking pools for the cattle droves which passed this way.

CORPSE ROAD
Continue uphill around a right bend and a left bend in the lane. From this last bend look for a blue-grey gate on the left. At the furthest end of the gate a narrow path can be seen between two hedges going away from the lane and down into a hollow. *This is the remains of the Gresford/Hawarden corpse road that I mentioned earlier when at Town Ditch.*

ROUTE B joins here

Continue along the lane. *At the farm track and house on the right, the fields opposite were called the Blue Field, Red Field, and White Field, and it was all to do with the dyeing of cloth in the 12th century. At the next left bend here is more evidence of the older road incorporated into*

40

a field system on the right. When the field is ploughed up to the hedge, the old cobble stones can be seen in the field along side the hedge.

After the bend, Cobblers Lane comes to a T junction with Dark Lane. *Opposite the junction there is a field gate, and this is the way the drove road originally went. The old right of way has been re-routed for some unknown reason.* Turn right and pass Lower Rackery. Opposite the old farmhouse is the gate to farm buildings and next to the gate is a very large bush. Immediately beyond this bush cross the hidden stile.

Go along the hedge on your left and cross the next stile at the rear of the farm buildings. Turn half-right past a small copse on the right, then through a partial boundary, straight across to the next stile towards the hall. *You are now back on the original route of the drove road. When this field was ploughed cobbles could be seen across the field.* From here continue, keeping the hedge on your left, until the path exits onto the B5373 Llay/Hawarden road. **For a bad weather shortcut or to avoid the mud in Gwasted Farm turn right along the main road then left at the next crossroads then follow the final two paragraphs of the route directions. If you take this shortcut you will miss some of the best parts of the drove road.**

RACKERY HALL
Diagonally opposite is Rackery Hall and a footpath finger post points the way along a drive and between the barns which have been converted to cottages. *Rackery Hall, built in the 17th century, had been re-used for an asylum, and in those days the B5373 was called Bedlam Lane. The Hall today and the buildings have all been refurbished and are now dwellings for private residents.*

Follow the path beside the garages to the rear where there is a gate and stone step stile. From the stile in the far hedge turn half-left across the field to the next stile then only slightly right across the open field. *Stop for a moment at the next hedge junction, for this hedge which comes from the hill on your right (Bryn-y-gaer) once bordered an old track, which joins the drove road that you are now standing on. The old track originally went to the hillfort on Bryn-y-gaer. Aerial photographs show prehistoric hut circles on the fields either side of this track. It makes you wonder just how old the drove road really is?*

41

Cross the stile and keep the hedge on your right to the next hedge and stile. *To the right of the stile there is a long avenue of trees: the original route of the drove road. Underneath the top soil the cobbles are intact. Lower down the avenue the road suddenly turns left to follow the next field hedge towards Gwasted Farm which is two fields to the south. This road should never have turned like this, and the reason lies in the fields beyond. There are several capped mine shafts. For in this area was a very large colliery and the old drove road was moved to go around these workings.*

GWASTED FARM

From this last stile the footpath goes sharp left diagonally across the next field. *In the corner of the field, by the brick drain, there is an awful lot of ground disturbance and this was caused by the removal of a railway which ran through two collieries and joined the main Bidston to Wrexham line at Caergwrle.* Go over the stile by the gate and follow the hedge on the left *which is now on the re-routed drove road.* At the next gate and stile, the path continues straight on between two hedges which still border the road. Gwasted Farm is to your left. *Stop at the top of a steep descent. The road went down as a hollow way and it is older than the re-routed drove road. This hollow way was the original entrance to Gwasted Farm from the drove road which we will see a bit later because the footpath has been re-routed.*

Go over the stile on your left. Go half-right. The path goes left around a border of trees to descend quite sharply into the River Alyn Valley towards the B5102 road and river bridge. From the stile in the corner go down a short steep section onto level ground then turn right along the path. *You are now on the wooded shoulder of the River Alyn Valley. If you look closely down the valley side you will see a terrace which is very overgrown with brambles and shrubs. This terrace climbs uphill to join the path that you are on. This is the remains of the original drove road from the ford on the Alyn. The ford was destroyed when the B5102 bridge was constructed.*

Continue along the path. *It was originally quite wide as you are now on the drove road and a section of Wat's Dyke. Keep an eye on the right hedge for it is moving further into the field away from the path. At a tree the hedge stops as if it has been cut off. From the tree there are three strands of wire which go across the direction of the path to another hedge on the left. It is through this gap the original drove once went. Look to the right and you will see the double hedge of the hollow way which went to Gwasted Farm. The remains of the drove road across the field have been completely obliterated.*

WAT'S DYKE

You are now on Wat's Dyke but only for a short distance as the path comes to a stile on the right which takes you off the dyke and into the lower fields. Go half-left across a concrete bridge and reinstated fields of the old colliery. Soon you will see a white cottage. Cross the next stile in the hedge to the right of the cottage. Fork left onto the path which goes past the cottage. *When the track bends slightly right you are once again on Wat's Dyke.* By some houses on the left the track joins Rhyddyn Hill. Turn left. *Opposite, there is a finger post pointing the way of a path over the shoulder of Bryn-y-gaer, this path is the continuation of Wat's Dyke as it goes behind Rhyddyn Farm.*

Go down Rhyddyn Hill. At the lower section of the lane keep on the left pavement past the mill and mill garden: an ideal resting place. Cross over the main road to the opposite pavement and turn left across the Alyn bridge. Go under the railway bridge and turn right into Castle Street. *Stop for a moment and look up to your left to a track on a shelf which services the houses up there. This track was the original village road before the construction of the present roads.* Continue up Castle Street around the left bend onto the pavement which will take you to the village Post Office and Spar shop where you started the walk.

THE END

Bewick Woodcut

43

ROUTE MAP
Not to scale

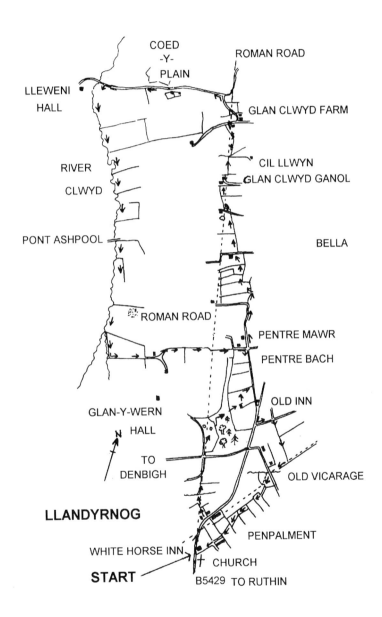

Roman & Medieval Roads
LLANDYRNOG (NORTHWEST)

START
The White Horse Inn SJ107652

ROUTE A   9 miles (14 kms)
The walk takes you along sections of the latter part of the Roman road which ran between Llandyrnog and Bodfari. Also included is a section of a medieval road from Rhuddlan Castle. The return route is a pleasant walk alongside the River Clwyd and a short walk along a Roman road which runs between Llandyrnog and the Afon Wen Pass.

ROUTE B   3 miles (5 kms)
The short route takes you along a section of the Bodfari Roman road and through a wooded landscape. It returns along part of a medieval road which once ran between Rhuddlan Castle and the Shropshire markets. Return through open fields and onto a section of the Afon Wen Roman road back to the village.

There are places where the Roman road goes over private land. This walk then uses parallel public paths but the route of the Roman road will be pointed out wherever possible.

HOW TO GET THERE
By Bus
There is a bus service which runs through the village between Denbigh and Ruthin.
By Car
Parking is available at The White Horse Inn in the village, **by request**.

See page 105 for directions from Mold, Denbigh and Ruthin.

HISTORY

The footpaths that you are about to walk have a history which goes back some eighteen hundred years. These paths were in use as roads and tracks up to the early seventeenth century. Any part of a Roman road which did not fit into the later systems was ploughed out leaving only a public right of way across the fields. As you are no doubt aware, footpaths have been moved since the early estates took over large tracts of land, thus giving the historian some problems in finding the exact route of the Roman road.

The Bodfari Roman road initially branched off the Chester to Corwen Roman road at Treuddyn (Mold). It travelled through Llanarmon-yn-Ial, Clwyd Gate Pass and then turned north to run along the east side of the Vale of Clwyd until reaching its final destination by joining the Denbigh to Bodfari Roman road. There are several names along the B5429 which give a clue to its presence. Names like: Stryt Mawr (Great Street), Penyffordd (Top of the road), Berth Elen* (Hedge Elen). The whole of the B5429 is not of Roman origin. It has taken several months to establish the course of the road between Plas-yn-rhos and Bodfari.

* Some historians say that the name 'Helen' refers to the Roman Emperor Macsen Wledig who took a Celtic wife named Elen (later corrupted to Helen) who lived at Caernarfon. She wanted her native home of Wales to have a fine network of roads, so her husband named them after her. If this is correct why are there not more roads in North Wales named 'HELEN'.

The explanation of William Condry in his book 'Snowdonia National Park' in which he says that Elen is a corruption of the words 'Y leng' which means 'of the legions' would be more befitting to the description of the Roman road network throughout Wales.

DIRECTIONS
ROUTE A & B

Leave the White Horse Inn, cross the main road to the bus shelter and turn right along the pavement. Go twenty metres and climb the stile on the left between a house and the village school. *This is the Roman Bodfari road. In the medieval period it became a road between Glan-y-wern Hall and the village church.*

White Horse Inn

PENISA' R-WAEN
Carry on into the field keeping to the school fence on your right. Go through the gate and follow the hedge on your left. At the end of the hedge the path goes down a gentle slope. Get over the stile directly ahead and immediately onto a footbridge over a stream. *On the 1873 First edition map there was a ford here not a footbridge.*

Continue along the footpath and keep to the hedge on your left. *This hedge is quite young in comparison to the other hedges round the fields: it has been planted in the last hundred years! This disguises the actual width of the old road, part of which is on the other side of the hedge. Halfway along the hedge there is a change in its structure: the trees and hawthorns are much older. Here is a noticeable hollow along the field perimeter parallel to the hedge. I have seen this on many occasions where the original Roman stone has been removed from a road that has gone out of use. The compression of the stones caused the hollow.*

47

Proceed into the second field and look for a stile on your left, alongside a tree. *You have now come to a medieval road junction. The track on your left was a medieval road between Glan-y-wern Hall and Pentre Llanrhaeadr.*

Resume the walk ahead and you will approach the rear of a modern farm building. Penisa'r-waen has been built across the line of the old road. Follow the present surfaced track around your right side of the building which is facing you, to where the road once again is much straighter and wider. This length is the original road which has been reinstated for the use of modern farm vehicles and the cottages which are on the left side of the lane. Continue until you reach the modern Denbigh road.

GLAN-Y-WERN HALL ESTATE
From the Penisa'r lane the footpath goes over the Denbigh road and onto the drive to Glan-y-wern Hall. On your right there is a modern bungalow. Find the stile which is at the end of the front garden fence. *Look along the hall drive to where it bends left by the first tree. Beyond this at the far hedge, you can see the tip of a large wood that spreads across to your right. The Roman road went from the drive entrance to the right side of the tree and passed close to the tip of this wood. The evidence of this is on aerial photographs. The Roman road now goes over private land. The footpath has been diverted away.*

WOODLAND WALK
The path follows the line of trees diagonally across the field. The path should enter the wood by a stile but there is only a piece of plastic on the fence. (You may have to use the gate to your left. Please shut it after you.) Inside the wood the right-of-way turns left to the track from the gate then right across a low level bridge. Turn half-right along the track. At the first bend, in only 35 metres, opposite a pond on your right, fork left through the woodland. At the field edge cross the ditch and fence into the field. Keep the cottage to your right. From the rear wall turn left and cross the centre of the field. Before the hedge turn right and continue to the lane. *The metalled lane was a medieval road which ran between Rhuddlan Castle and the Shropshire markets.*

ROUTE B   Turn right. Go to page 53

ROUTE A
PENTRE-MAWR

Turn left. *On your left you soon pass the rusty brick farm buildings of Pentre-Mawr Hall. Part of the building facing you has been turned into two small cottages. Past these buildings and on the left is the old hall encircled by trees. The hall has been handed down through the family for years. They once owned all the land between Llandyrnog and Bodfari.*

Continue along the lane as it seems to wander aimlessly between its borders of trees and shrubs for the next quarter of a mile. Where the tarmac surface ends go through the fieldgate ahead (please shut it after you) and resume your walk between the hedge and trees which border the green road. Follow it round a right bend and a left bend and then look for a stile on your left. *You are now leaving the medieval road.* Turn half-right and proceed to a field gate which can be seen in the far hedge. ***Stop for a moment and look left to the hedge lower down the field. The hedge borders the Roman road. Please do not go there as you will be trespassing, there is not a lot to see, unless you know what to look for. You will get the chance to see the road a bit further on.***

Beyond the field gate follow the hedge on your right to another stile to enter some woods.

WARNING
If you have an OS map, you may notice on it that there is a path indicated along the lower hedge. This path has been closed down by the County Council and re-routed, you are now on the replacement path.

GLANCLWYD-BELLA
Wander through the woods along the path until reaching a footbridge and stile from which you go straight across the field to cross a stile alongside a lane. Turn left and walk twenty-five metres to a stile on your right.

THE ROMAN ROAD
Now is your chance to see an actual piece of the Roman road. Go past this stile and follow the lane passing Glanclwyd Bella. Go round a left bend and a right bend. Where the lane turns right into a smallholding, there is a rusty field gate directly ahead of you. (This is a public footpath.)

49

Go through this gate onto a very overgrown green road and in 25 metres take the gateway on your left into the narrow field above a deep wooded gully. (This is not a recorded public right of way so if asked to leave you should explain that you are just looking at the Roman road and then return to the path.) Follow the fall of the land to a fence. To your right there is a stile, ignore this, turn left and go along the fence to a hedge. *Now look over the fence and down the steep side of the gully, you will see the remains of a terrace ascending from the depths. This is the Roman road. Originally it was three metres wide but erosion has reduced it.*

What you cannot see is, on the opposite side of the gully, where the Roman road looks like a wide deep ditch running down to the stream below. A landowner has turned all the ditches into it. The action of water running over the stony surface has eventually cut through, forming a channel. There had been a ford but with the lack of maintenance this has been washed away. Only the clues either side remain. Wooded gullies like this are an ideal place to find the existence of a Roman road, untouched by the plough and modern farming methods, only to be eroded by time and weather.

Return the way you came until you reach the stile on the left, opposite Glanclwyd Bella.

CIL LLWYN

Step over the stile and turn right to follow the fence on your right along the field. *Halfway down the field look to your left where there is a high ridge of ground. Between you and the ridge there are deep marks in the ground surface running parallel with the path. This is all that remains of the Roman road.*

At the far end of the second field go beside the boulder and cross the narrow gravel track. Continue straight across the fields. You will arrive at a stile and steps down onto the access drive at the front of Glan Clwyd Ganol. Cross the drive and go through a field gate into the field at the side of the farmhouse. Carry on to the stile set in the hedge. *Beyond this stile you are on the Roman road. Look carefully under the overhanging hedge and you will see lots of sandstone chips and small stones. The farmer said that when he ploughed within three metres of the hedge the ground surface was a long line of small rounded stones along the footpath. (The sandstone chips may have been placed on the road surface in a later period.)*

Use two stiles to pass the pond. *Look to your right in between them and there you will see a narrow track which has gone out of use. It is tracks like this that give the clue to the whereabouts of a Roman road. The track goes to Cil Llwyn Farm, which was the original entrance to the farm. There is a later entrance road, which is on the other side of the farm, that goes to the medieval road. We know that the Normans constructed roads across the country (medieval roads). The Romans were the only ones to build a large scale system of roads before the Normans, so the older entrance track may go to a Roman road. In this case it did.*

GLAN CLWYD

In the field turn right, the landowner has had permission to change the route of the path to follow the field boundaries. Follow the hedge on your right then turn left beside the fence until you cross the stile halfway along. Follow the fence, now on your left, until you reach the corner of the field. Here you turn right to cross a stile alongside a field gate on your left. *Stop for a moment on the narrow lane. The Roman road which crossed the previous field has been completely obliterated, even aerial photographs are of no help. The only way to find where it may have been on the latter field is to backtrack from another section. The next piece of the Roman road was found alongside a later farm track which leaves Glan Clwyd Farm. The farm is further along the lane to your right. With this find and a hypothetical line placed on a map to the length by Cil Llwyn entrance track, the Roman road was discovered to have passed between you and the houses that you can see to the right.*

HOLY ROAD

A small diversion can be made here to see the holy road. Turn left along the lane. A notice on the entrance gate says 'strictly private'. Carry on, this is an illegal notice: this road is a county highway as far as the next bend. When the lane bends look through the fieldgate ahead onto the remains of an old grass track running between trees. This track was a holy road, sometimes known as a monks' way, which ran between the Denbigh Abbey and the Holywell Abbey. This book was going to use it to the river until it was discovered that the next section is no longer *recorded as a public road or footpath. Return up the lane to the stile. Ignore the next direction `Turn right` and continue ahead.*

GLAN-CLWYD

Turn right. Before the farmhouse, turn left along the first gated farm track. In the field remain on the track to the T junction. *The Roman road runs alongside the hedge to your right. It heads under the A55 and the dismantled railway then continues below the foothills to join the Denbigh/Lixwm Roman road which was later re-used for coaches.*

Turn left and follow the metalled track between two mature lime trees. Beyond the cattle grid continue along the track then turn left along the river. *Note the old course of the river and the old stone bridge. Along the river bank count the number of wild fowl that you see. I saw nine different species.*

THE SWIMMER

It was along this river that I found out that squirrels can swim. I had sat down to eat my lunch when there was an almighty splash from under the overhanging branches over the river. Thinking that it was a large fish, I did not really take much interest, until I saw a little head and body swimming like the devil to the river bank. A squirrel climbed out looking slightly wet, sitting up on its haunches. It gave itself a good shake, looked at me, and then ran up a tree as fast as it could go.

GLAN-Y-WERN

Continue along the river bank until you reach a farmer's bridge across the river. *On the OS map this is called Pont Ashpool. (Ashpool bridge). Plas Ashpool (Ashpool Hall) is a mile away on the B5429.* Carry on past the bridge until you come to the third stile in a field corner by a right bend in the river, this stile has platform steps. From here go fifty metres and there is another stile alongside a field gate. Ignore this and follow the fence along a deep ditch to another fence. In the corner of the fences there is a stile, ignore this as well, turn left and continue with the fence on your right. Directly ahead you will see a field gate and a stile. Glan-y-wern Farm can be seen above the river meadow to your right.

Beyond the stile you will enter a narrow field access track which ascends through woods passing a brick cattle shelter on your left. At the bend in

52

the track there is a stone wall. Go left here to a stile in the corner. Follow the hedge on your left going up the field, go over another stile and continue along the fenced hedge. *When you come to a trough on the left, count forty metres ahead and stop. This is where the Roman road went across the fields (shown on aerial photographs).*

Resume your walk to the top of the field. Cross the stile in the corner and continue along the lane ahead to the crossroad. Turn right.

TO LLANDYRNOG   ROUTE A & B

Continue along the medieval road until it meets with the B5429. *Prior to the construction of the B road, the medieval road went straight across the fields ahead of you and past the Kimmel Arms and Vicarage which you will see later. The modernised cottage on your left at the junction of the roads was originally the Cross Keys Inn, a seventeenth century building, one more reminder of the previous crossing.*

Turn right along the modern road. Turn first left and follow the lane uphill until reaching a narrower lane on the left. Opposite there is a field gate and footpath. At the time of writing it was impossible to open the gate and it had to be climbed. Follow the hedge on your right. The next stile is at the next corner, difficulties here have been reported to the Highway Authority. *I have called this footpath the rabbit run because there is an abundance of rabbits living along the hedge. In the second field look to your right. You will see the rear of the Kimmel Arms and the very stylish former Vicarage which are alongside the medieval road.*

THE AFON WEN ROAD

Go over the stile in the right corner of the field and follow the hedge on the left towards the Creamery chimney. *You are now on another Roman road which came from Caerwys, through the Afon Wen Pass, which goes through Llandyrnog to Llanrhaeadr on the west side of the Rivers Clwyd and Clwyedog. If you look closely under the left hedge you will see some of the stones from the old road. Under the grass surface, 300mm below the road, stones are still in place.*

Follow the path into the next field then go between the stream and the outer boundary of the old vicarage. Turn slightly left, and cross the stream to a stile alongside the medieval road. Go over the stile opposite and continue along the hedge on the right until you reach a hollow going uphill to your left. *This hollow is the remains of the Roman road. It forded the stream and turned uphill to the crest to make another re-alignment. Roman roads only turned or re-aligned on or at fords and crests of hills. The road re-aligned for a purpose. If it had continued straight on it would have gone into marshy ground. Unfortunately you will not see this marshy ground now because the CO-OP constructed a large milk bottling factory over this particular area.*

Turn left along the hollow uphill. *This road is also along part of an old parish boundary. At the crest the road re-aligned west, and the boundary went straight on. There is no evidence of the Roman road going west from the hilltop because it probably has been ploughed out, but its route will be pointed out to you lower down the fields.*

Continue past the tall trees and go directly ahead to a hedge where you will find a stile leading onto an enclosed footpath. *This path was kept clear by the local Authority up to last year, but perhaps due to cut-backs in their budget, it is now getting overgrown.*

Across the next field the stile is directly ahead alongside a field gate. Continue onto a field access to the next stile. *At the end of the enclosed track stop and look to your right.*

PENPALMENT
There is a field gate in the lower field to the rear of the milk factory, this is where the Roman road was. When I was there the field was being ploughed and there was a long line of stones across the field indicating the route of the road.

Now look over to the hedge which borders the white farmhouse and a field gate, this is where the Roman road went through. In the farmyard it has been destroyed by later farm buildings. The name of the farm is Penpalment, in English this means top or end of the pavement, it is not referring to the pavement alongside the B5429 on the otherside of the farm. It refers to a Roman road, the surface of the road whether it was slabs or small stones rammed into a hard material, was called a pavement. Any building or farm with a name like this is usually on a Roman road.

54

Go slightly left along the fence to the next stile. Continue ahead to a stile in the hedge at the rear of the council houses. Follow the path to the White Horse Inn.

THE END

Toll Tariff from the Bala - Dolgellau Road

ROUTE MAP
Not to scale

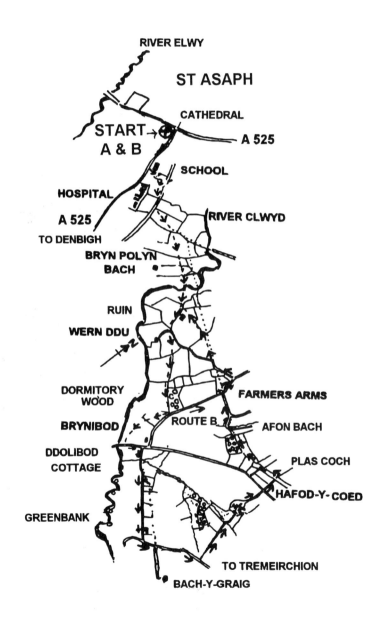

Medieval Roads
ST ASAPH

START
Cathedral   SJ036743

St Asaph Cathedral

ROUTE A   7 miles (11 kms)
This is a circular walk along a medieval road and through an abundance of wildlife. It returns along another medieval road and a Roman one.

ROUTE B   4 miles (7 kms)
This shortcut leaves the main route after 2 miles.

HOW TO GET THERE

By Bus

Services run from Denbigh and Rhyl.

By Car

St Asaph is well-signposted. The cathedral car park is for visitors only but there is a car park at the foot of the High Street, by the river.

DIRECTIONS

From the Cathedral go along the Denbigh road A525. Pass the school on the opposite side and take the footpath (signposted) beside the Sport and Leisure Centre. Beyond the brick bungalow `Avola` go around the football pitch to the far corner where a well-worn path negotiates around some bushes onto the old railway track. Go over the stile immediately on the right and walk along the track to the ruins of a bridge. Here, climb the low embankment to a kissing gate. In the field turn half-right and follow the path across the slope towards a lone oak tree by the next stile. *Look across to the opposite side of the River Clwyd valley where a farm track leaves the river area and goes towards Rhewl Farm. This is the remains of the St Asaph Roman road to Holywell.*

Proceed, keeping the hedge on the right, until reaching a field gate and another tree. Turn half-left and go down and across the slope to a small footbridge and the next stile. Follow the same line across the next field towards a field gate. *Look down into the lower meadow immediately below the slope. Here are the faint remains of a track which runs southeast towards a bend on the river just below the present footbridge. This is the St Asaph branch to the main medieval road on the opposite side of the river.*

Carry on along the path to the River Clwyd footbridge. *Once over the bridge, pause for a moment and look left to a hedge which runs from the river bend and up the old river embankment. On this bank the hedge is at its thickest and it hides an old road cutting which is now a hollow for a stream. At the top of the bank the remains of the road disappear. On the OS 1893 First Edition map a narrow road is shown to run from the northeast side of Rhewl Farm, along this embankment and south towards Wern Ddu farm. This was the medieval road's original route. Naturally, with the lack of use, the road has been ploughed out; even the right of way has been removed.*

From the footbridge go straight up the meadow to a field gate and then towards a field hedge keeping the ruins on your left. Do not take the footpath which goes left. Turn half-right and continue with the tall hedge on your left. Cross the stile by a field gate at the top of the field, pass caravans and go to the lane. Take the steps leading up to a stile. *The footpath is a re-route over the hill to the left of the Wern Ddu Farm: the original road went through it.*

Proceed over the top of the hill and down to another stile. Keeping a fence and hedge on the left, continue downhill past the nicely laid out gardens of Ysgolis House. Beyond the gardens ignore the track which goes to the left. The stile is in the hedge directly ahead. *After going through Wern Ddu the medieval road came to this point. The only evidence of the road is in the first field on leaving the farm, the remainder of the road has been ploughed out.*

Go over the stile and walk alongside Dormitory Wood. *At this point you are very close to the River Clwvd. There is a lot of activity along this stretch of the river where wild ducks are continually landing and taking off. Do birds know when someone is nearby with a camera? I wanted some pictures and they all vanished at once. Across the river to the west is Llannerch Hall. During autumn in the early morning sun the Virginia Creeper which covers the southern wall is ablaze with a bright orange colour; a contrast to the remaining autumn landscape.*

ROUTE B
At the modern road cross the stone stile and turn left. Follow the road.
Now go to page 63

Now go to page 63

BRYN IBOD
At the modern road ignore the stone stile in the roadside wall, but turn right and stay inside the field (this is the footpath although it has sometimes been illegally cropped). At the next field gate the path turns half-right (southwest) to a piece of sheep-cropped pasture which has not seen a plough. *On the hill top to the left is Bryn Ibod.* Continue downhill where the footpath has now taken the appearance of a road: *the original Waen road.* The footpath exits onto the modern Trefnant road prior to the Clwyd river bridge. Turn left and keep on the right side of the main road

until reaching a small lane on the right. *Look at Bryn Ibod on the hill: you will see the old road descending to fall onto line with this lane.*

Medieval Road at Bryn Ibod

GREENBANK

The start of the lane is surfaced. It goes over a small bridge to Ddolibod Cottage, the lane then becomes purely grass and cobbles. In places it is overgrown but horse riders have made it easier to get through. *From the cottage the lane climbs slightly uphill and then there is a silly bend to the right, which made me curious as to why. Because at the further end of the lane it meets the later Denbigh road. The continuation of the road is on the opposite side and is a field away to the left (surely the medieval builders would not stagger a road like this). There is a clue by Greenbank Farm. The surface of the lane changes, there are no cobbles under the modern spread. The original course was probably changed when the later Tremeirchion/Denbigh road was constructed.*

60

GREENBANK FARM

In a kilometre go through Greenbank Farm. *With permission for exploration in the fields above and on the east side of the farm it was soon established that the medieval road had once followed the upper field hedge, as cobbles could be found beneath the hedges, too many to have been picked off the fields.* This is where I got nearly run down by charging horses and a too friendly goat who decided that a butt or two on my rump would help me on my way rather rapidly.

Leave Greenbank and turn left along the Tremeirchion Road. In a short distance there is a drive on the right before Coed Duon. *On your left there is a short field access, this was the original route of the medieval road. It goes down the drive to your right through Bach-y-graig. Due to a disastrous series of errors by the Highway Authority and the Parish Council in the 1950s when the Rights-of-way map was drawn, public paths in Bach-y-graig do not connect through the property so this is where we must stop following the medieval road. It originally continued eastwards and has been reused as access for Hendre Farm, near Bodfari, before going across the fields beyond. Any evidence of the next part of the road has been destroyed by the Denbigh/Mold coach road which once ran between the later railway and the farm.*

The road can be found again slightly west of Aberwheeler and follows the present day lanes and footpaths through Llandrynog to the southern end of the Clwyd Vale where it meets other roads from West Wales on their way to Chester, Whitchurch and Oswestry.

THE RETURN

Continue along the road. In half a kilometre turn left along a drive.

HAFOD-Y-COED

At the cottage continue through gates ahead. As you approach the hall look for a small black gate on your left. Go along the path beside the fence. Pass an ornamental pool on your left and go to the stile in the comer of the garden. Do not go over this stile but turn right keeping the garden railings on your left. The path goes along the edge of the gardens past the hall on your right. Proceed along the drive until reaching the lodge on your left, and the Tremeirchion/Trefnant road.

PLAS COCH

Opposite the lodge there is a track. *This was the continuation of the original drive from Hafod-y-Coed Hall prior to the construction of the Tremeirchion/Trefnant road. The drive once connected to the Tremeirchion/St Asaph medieval road.* Follow it through a gate. *You are now standing on the original medieval road. In the fields to the right it has been ploughed out. To the left, there is a large cattle shed built on it.* Continue straight on through another gate into a field. Turn left and continue with the hedge on the left which goes past the rear of the cattle shed through a pylon.

AFON BACH

Continue past Plas Coch Farm to the large hedge on the left. *This is the continuation of the medieval road. The majority of the road has been ploughed out leaving only a hollow as a reminder of its presence. Only the side ditch remains which takes waste water from the farm down the sloping fields of the Afon Bach (small river).*

Fork left into the field with the pylons and remain beside the hedge and ditch. *By a wooded area the ditch becomes wider as it starts a steeper decline into the vale. Along this section the remains of the Roman road from Bodfari to St Asaph can be seen. The road has been well used, the length along the brook side being much worn down. This is probably due to the type of vehicles that have used it since Roman times. In the fifteenth century many of the early farm carts did not have wheels, only a type of wooden skids.*

At a crossing fence go over the broken stile. Continue downhill through a small plantation. A small gate opens onto the track. It is the entrance drive to Glanrafon Cottage which is upstream. Turn left along this drive and over the iron river bridge. Follow the track round a right hand bend out of the valley. *Halfway up look over the right hedge and you will see the Roman road parallel to the track that you are standing on.* Turn left at Ty-Gwyn Cottage. *The cottage has been built on top of the Roman road. Evidence of this can be seen in the rear garden. Halfway along the lane the Roman road and the modern lane combine.* Walk to the T junction with the Waen Trefnant road. *Originally the Roman road went straight across into the opposite fields here. We will see a short section of the old road soon.* Turn right along the modern road.

ROUTE B rejoins here

Pass the Farmers Arms on your right. Just beyond the next house turn left into the Wern Ddu lane. Follow it to the first right bend by Plas-yn-Cornel. *This is where the Roman road originally came out from the fields. Today a short section has been re-used for the surfaced lane. If you look carefully at the hedge where the road originally came through you will notice a difference in the height of the ditch bank The hedge itself is an implant and the field leading to this hedge has been disturbed so much that no evidence of the old road remains.*

FINAL STAGE
Continue straight along the road until the next sharp bend left. Continue ahead on the footpath to the gate and stile on the far side of the field. *An outline of the road can be seen to the right of the field gate, further into the field it disappears.*

Carry on across the next field keeping the hedge on the left until a crossing fence and a stile with concrete steps down onto a lower field. Keep the hedge on your left. In 30 metres take the stile beside the gate on your left. The ruins are on your left. From here-on you will rejoin the outward route. It is only a short walk back to the river footbridge and St Asaph.

THE END

Bewick Woodcut

ROUTE MAP
Not to scale

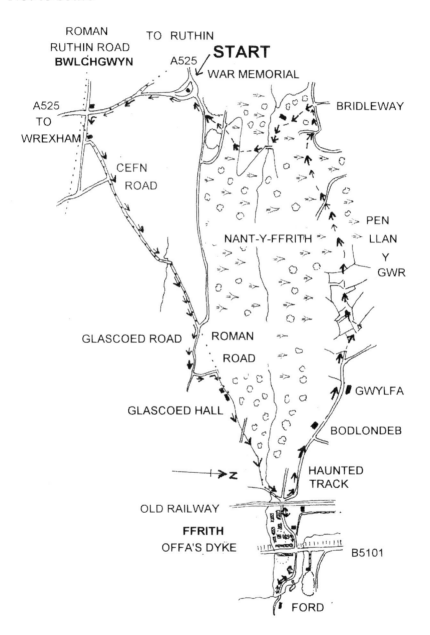

A Roman Road to Ffrith
BWLCHGWYN

START
War Memorial **SJ 263537**

ROUTE 9 miles (14 Kms)
Half the route is downhill.

HOW TO GET THERE
By Bus
The Wrexham/Gwynfryn service goes through Bwlchgwyn.
By Car
The War Memorial is situated on the A525 Wrexham/Ruthin Road. There is car parking space beside it.

HISTORY
Ffrith is a small village nestled in a picturesque valley northwest of Wrexham. In the Roman period it was a large working settlement. Historians have searched for years attempting to find a road that would link the complex to the large fort at Chester (Deva). During this search several other roads came to light. The road that you are about to walk was a main road which, after leaving Ffrith, passed through Bwlchgwyn and continued to a settlement at Ruthin. Since the Roman period there have been many changes to the existing road system. First the Saxons used one Roman road as a base for Offa's Dyke. Later came the packhorse trains who used one of the Roman ditches alongside a road. The appearance of the packhorse trails would alter considerably. In and around Bwlchgwyn there has been a substantial amount of quarrying through the different periods, and the roads have been diverted to suit these quarries. Ever since the invention of the motor car, roads are being changed to enable vehicles to go faster. The course of the Ffrith/Ruthin road through Bwlchgwyn has been modernised, but the majority of it is either under a present day road or very close to it. Wherever possible this guide attempts to explain where the old road is.

Why change or construct another road when there is a good road already there? There are several reasons for this. When the Romans left our shores people settled down and very few travelled from place to place, leaving the travelling to traders like those that ran the packhorse trains either buying from or selling wares to the farms. Another reason is that houses were built on the road, for it provided a good foundation. There are several roads like this where not one house but a whole row of dwellings are built along the road.

If a road has not been used for a couple of years it just vanishes beneath leaves and grass. When a new road was required no-one had the time to find the course of the old one or had forgotten that it had existed. It was far quicker to build another road. The large estates closed a lot of the old main routes down. Not wanting a main road through their land they paid for the coach roads and turnpikes to be re-routed around the estate walls. There have been quite a few Roman roads traced through estates in North Wales. Nowadays the landowners seem to be quite pleased that they have something unique and so old on their property.

DIRECTIONS
From the Memorial go south along the A525 Wrexham road keeping the Nant-y-Ffrith valley to your rear. Walk along the left pavement passing the Westminster Arms on your right until you reach the Kings Head Inn on the right. *Alongside the inn is Fron Heulog Hill. This lane replaced the Ffrith/Ruthin Roman road.* Turn left into Brymbo Road opposite. Keep on the left pavement. *Stop when you are opposite Bwlchgwyn School and by Cefn Road on your left. The Brymbo Road is a replacement for the Roman road which can be seen in the field opposite the cottages further downhill. Exactly where it went at Brymbo remains unsolved, as the steel works destroyed all traces.*

Turn left into Cefn Road. *The house immediately on your left has been built across a Roman road.* Continue round the right-hand bend. *You are now on the Ffrith/Ruthin Roman road. On the early maps this road was called The Ridgeway and that is exactly where it runs, along a ridge over a hill.*

Follow the lane over the hill and down to the stream. *If you study the hedge system here you can see that the lane had once been considerable*

66

wider at this point. Improvements to the present lane have reduced its original width.

Continue along the lane until it meets the Glascoed Road, where you turn right and go downhill. *Originally the Roman road went straight across the field on your left. Why change the system? The first reason is that there were, and still are, two springs in the field. These were close to the old road in the field, and probably through the lack of maintenance, the trail had become very wet and boggy. Humans have a habit of walking around large muddy areas and creating extra roads. On the aerial photographs these additional tracks can be seen clearly.*

The second reason is that a lot of these older lanes were unsuitable for the collection of milk and cattle from the large farms during two world wars. During these times POWs were used to construct more suitable lanes enabling vehicles to get to the individual farms. The Roman road did not meet this criteria.

An old road is a public right of way. Even in war time roads would not be closed down if a section was re-routed. This is exactly what happened to the section across the field: the re-route will be found lower down Glascoed Road on the left, signposted as a bridleway.

Turn left onto the bridleway and follow it to a sharp right bend. *If you look carefully at the hedge on your left, you will see that there has been an implant which closed off access where the original track came through.* Turn right and proceed down the bridleway. Look on you right at the large holly trees. These have been planted here by the landowner to shield the rear of Glascoed Hall from users of the old road.

Lower down the bridleway and at the immediate rear of the farm buildings the track descends quite rapidly on a slight right bend and then levels out again. *This bend has been caused by farm buildings encroaching along the edge of the track. On the level there is another bend to the left, this time the curve was caused by the insertion of a field system on your left.*

The road now starts to descend once more, and here a later bridge has been constructed over it. *The bridge was used by vehicles going to and fro from a nineteenth century stone quarry higher up in the valley.* Leaving the bridge, the track narrows and levels out until it reaches the shoulder of the valley. From here the bridleway takes on the appearance of a typical packhorse trail, well worn down into a deep groove with high sides. This is where the track curves slightly left and right returning onto a level section. *Here, look to your right and you will see another road which has not been so well used. This is the Roman road and it is obvious that the packhorses used the outer ditch.*

Finally the track plunges down a much steeper section until reaching an even level along the side of the Nant-y-Ffrith River. *Look carefully at the field on your right and you will see that it was once divided up into smaller field systems which are possibly from the Roman period.* Continue until you meet another track from the right. This is the quarry road that crossed over the bridge that you passed under. Turn left then follow the track round to the right and through the arch of a spectacular disused railway viaduct. *The railway had been a mineral line which ran between Wrexham and Denbigh, collecting ores from the large quarries. The railway was finally closed when it became cheaper to transport the ore by road.*

Crying his wares   *Bewick Woodcut*

68

FFRITH

Continue along the modern road to pass through the council estate. You have now entered the village of Ffrith. Continue to the Blue Bell Inn. *Stop for a moment and look to your right at the rear of the terraced cottages which are alongside the modern main road and the council houses which are to the rear of these. When the council houses were being built a large circular Roman complex was found and it stretches underneath the cottages alongside the modern road. This working complex was for making artefacts which were distributed to the various Roman towns in the northwest. It is not unusual for local people digging in their gardens to find Roman coins and other remains.*

THE FORD

Leave the inn and cross the modern road.. *You have now just crossed Offa's Dyke: the modern road was constructed along it in 1828 when a hoard of Roman coins, silver and beads were found.* Continue along the Cymau road which goes alongside a large playing field on your right. At the lower part of the road there is a stone bridge on your left. *This was a packhorse bridge over the River Cegidog. (See:A Packhorse Trail and a Drovers' Road.)*

Packhorse Bridge

69

Resume your walk along the road until you reach the shallow ford. *This is comparatively modern. It was constructed to enable motor vehicles to reach the cottages on the opposite side. To the front of these cottages there is a track which goes uphill: this is the continuation of the road and packhorse trail which goes to the village of Cymau and Caergwrle. It is not a Roman road.*

Return the way you came. At the modern road turn right onto the bridge. **Look at the entrance to the cottage between you and the Poachers Inn on your side of the modern road. On old maps this entrance was called Lime Stryt. I believe that this was originally the Roman road to Caergwrle, which has been destroyed by later quarrying to the rear of the cottage. Sections of this road can be found on higher ground to the northwest side of the village of Cymau. Other roads leave the Roman complex north and south.**

Cross the modern road to the Blue Bell Inn and stop on the track to the right of the inn. *This is a road that goes north to Caerwys. After the right bend there is a Joinery Works. When the owner of this works expanded by excavating part of the hill to the rear of the property, there were two kilns found intact. Either side of these kilns there was a vertical layer of a concrete-like substance which retained the rock face of the hillside. On trying to remove this, three mechanical picks broke down. Eventually it was removed, but only by blasting it away from the rock face.*

THE GHOST

Now go back the way you entered the village and under the railway viaduct. Fork right up the track. It rises steeply and bends to the left. *This track, prior to the construction of the railway and station went straight down into the village. Proceed uphill and you will notice that although the track is deep and narrow. There are no level sections like the previous track on the opposite side of the Nant-y-Ffrith. This track is of a later period and not Roman times.*

As you walk uphill under the canopy of the trees, you may feel a chill in the air. If you are with a party of fellow walkers and some start being awkward and argumentative, it is not their fault, it is the presence of a ghost!

A local tale relates that at the top of the hill two brothers lived in a small cottage. One was mild tempered and easy going, worked hard and saved every penny. The other was completely opposite in character, always drinking and spending his money. When arguments broke out the noise could be heard throughout the valley.

One afternoon there was a lot of shouting. Normally the locals would shrug their shoulders because they had got used to this daily row but on this day the shouting seemed to be coming closer and louder. The brothers could be heard fighting on the track and stones came rattling down the trail as if some earthquake had loosened them. The locals knew that it would not be wise to interfere, for when these two men fought, anyone who tried to pull them apart was set upon by the brothers.

Haunted Track

71

Suddenly the row stopped as if a switch had been pulled, peace befell the valley. The locals could not understand this sudden silence. Curiosity overcame them and somehow they raised the courage to venture up the track. They found the first brother lying in a pool of blood with his throat cut. Further up the track the second brother was wedged against a tree, a knife buried deep in his back, quite dead. They carried the bodies back to

the cottage and set it on fire so that the brothers were cremated with all their worldly goods. Ever since that day anyone who uses the track seems to start arguing at that particular point.

After leaving the trees the track meets a surfaced lane. Continue straight uphill. *There is a modernised cottage on your left named Bodlondeb. This is supposed to be the site of the brothers' cottage. There have never been ghosts felt here.*

PEN-LLAN-Y-GWR.
Beyond Gwylfa. Where the lane bends right and starts to drop follow the old quarry track (signposted) up to your left. Beyond the gate and stile it zigzags its way up the hill. *On each turn of the track there is either the remains of a building or just a building platform. In the late eighteenth century this was a busy quarry. Look to your right and left as the track makes its way uphill towards the woodland. On both sides of the track there can be seen the remains of stone circles, these may have been hut circles or the remains of cairns. The hill is named Pen-Llan-y-Gwr (top enclosure of man) and may refer to the stone circles. Behind you is the Dee Estuary. To your right, on the horizon, is the ruined Jubilee Tower on the top of Moel Famau; to your left, across the valley, is the remaining stump of Brymbo Bottle Chimney once used for lead smelting. Beyond that is the Cheshire plain.*

Go over the stiles and into the woods. Follow the path up to the rocky viewpoint then continue downhill. Where it breaks out of the trees a large expanse of timber has been cleared to your left and the footpath has been widened for the use of forestry vehicles. When the widened path joins a level forest road, turn right and walk 12 metres, then turn left onto the continuation of the footpath which threads its way through the trees. *You will notice that this path is quite wide and has a wall on either side, for it is the remains of an estate road.* Follow it downhill and do not turn off it.

72

The track eventually breaks out onto a forest road. Do not turn left or right but continue straight on. Stay on the forest road as it descends until it comes to a gate. Go through the gate and walk 28 metres then turn left onto a bridleway. Follow this downhill passing the lodge house on the right until you reach a field gate which says "End of bridleway". Cross the stile on the right in the fence, then go left along the driveway to cross the bridge on the right.

NANT-Y-FFRITH VALLEY

You are now in the Nant-y-ffrith Valley. It was once owned by a man named Kyrke, an Ironmaster of the 19th century, who later bought the Hall here which has since been demolished. The valley was planted out with exotic trees and shrubs. If you look carefully amid the pines you will see these trees and shrubs that still grow here. One of the residents of the hall was Kyrke's daughter who became the first white woman to cross the Andes.

JOURNEY'S END

From the end of the wall on your right walk 16 metres, a footpath can be found threading its way uphill through the trees. Stay on this path until you reach a forest track. Turn right for 8 metres and turn left to continue uphill along the path. On reaching the green road go straight on uphill to the stile onto the lane. Go straight across onto an old quarry track and, where the track is about to enter the quarry, bear left onto a path which rises quite sharply uphill alongside the quarry on your right. When the path exits onto the Glascoed Road, turn right and, after a short walk, you are back at the memorial.

THE END

Bewick Woodcut

ROUTE MAP
Not to scale

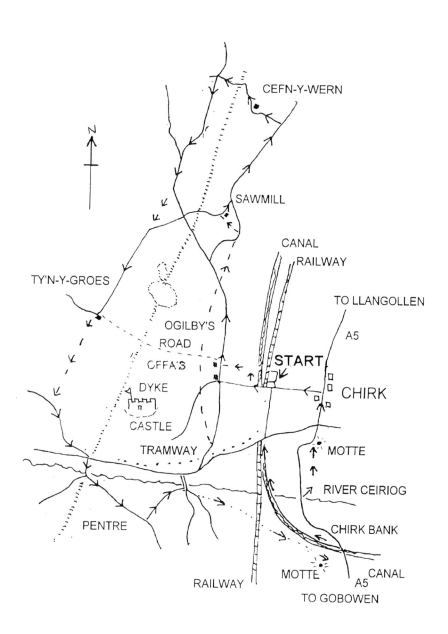

Ogilby's Chester to Cardiff Road
CHIRK

START
Chirk Station SJ284377

ROUTE A 8 miles (13 kms) *for the brave which includes heights and a tunnel.*
ROUTE B 8 miles (13 kms) *for the not so brave avoiding the aqueduct and tunnel.*

The walk uses an interesting route around the perimeter of Chirk Castle covering a part of the old Chester to Cardiff road and some of the roads marked on his map. The route takes you through a landscape formed by man down the ages.

HOW TO GET THERE
By Train
Chirk is on the Wrexham/ Shrewsbury line.
By Bus
The village is on the Wrexham/Oswestry route. The railway station is along Station Avenue (opposite the Hand Inn) which leads to the main entrance of Chirk Castle.
By Car
Chirk is signposted from the A5 bypass. The railway station is along Station Avenue (opposite the Hand Inn) which leads to the main entrance of Chirk Castle. Parking is available at the station.

HISTORY
In 1675, John Ogilby, `Cosmographer` to King Charles II published a book of highway routes between major cities with the first 1 inch to 1 mile scale. One of his routes mapped the main Chester to Cardiff road. After passing through Ruabon by `ye Colepitts`. The road crossed the `New bridge` (beside the present bridge of the same name) across the `Dee flu` (River Dee). It made its way through Pentre (on what is now a

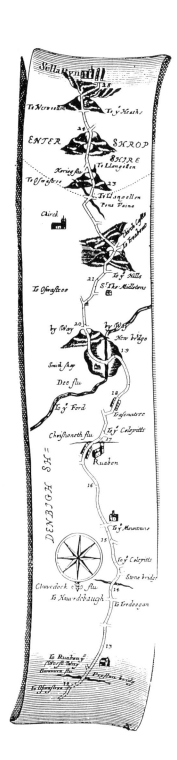

Part of John Ogilby`s
Chester to Cardiff route

76

public footpath) and beside Cefn-y-wern, owned by Sir Thomas Middleton of Chirk Castle. It then crossed the castle parkland. Like many estate owners, the Middletons diverted the road outside their walls in the 18th century and, in this case built the wall across it. The hollow-way can still be found crossing the Permissive Summer Path, and at the first right bend of the entrance drive. The road then descended the track above `Pont Vaine` (Pont Faen) to cross the Keriog flu (River Ceiriog) and headed for Selattyn past `Werwoolm` (Wern wool mill). Many parts of the road are now just footpaths or bridleways. This route only follows a small part of Ogilby's road as much is now on private land.

This part of Ogilby's Road is to the left of the first right bend as the old road crosses the entrance drive. It can be seen when the castle is open. There is no charge if you walk up the driveway.

77

DIRECTIONS ROUTE A & B

From the railway station turn right and cross the railway bridge. *There are two bridges here. The first is for the railway; the second crosses the former course of the Glyn Valley Tramway. In 1888 the tramway was re-routed from its south of Chirk Bank to run alongside the Great Western Railway Station. The unusual 1/2 gauge track, originally built at 2 feet 4 1/2 inches (71.6cm) and changed slightly for steam, ran 10 kilometres to the station at Glyn Ceiriog, with extensions to the mines and quarries of that area. Slate, china clay, granite, tarmacadam, flannel and passengers were transported until 1933 when, due to heavy losses, only goods were carried. The final closure of the line was in 1935.*

Now follow the road past the turning for the industrial estate and over the canal bridge to the footpath signposted on your right. Follow the path through the woods and fork left after 50 metres. Cross the next stile and go up the field to a stile alongside a lane. Turn right. *When the permissive summer path is open, go up to beyond the second stile. A deep hollow way is the original medieval road from the village to the castle. A little further uphill, filled in with rubble, Ogilby`s road can be seen crossing it. If you go to look return to this lane to continue the walk.* Continue along the lane as far as the sharp left-hand bend after two large oaks. Climb the stile up on your right. *You are now on part of the Chester to Cardiff road mapped by John Ogilby in 1675. The road in those days would be nothing more than a dirt track. It originally ran into the grounds of Chirk Castle opposite the stile but the estate has now been enclosed and a wall built over the road.*

You reach a lane. *This part of the old road has become a tarmac lane.* Cross the stile opposite. Follow the footpath across the field. When you reach the narrow lane, turn right. *The cottage on your right is a listed building and a former sawmill.* At the road junction turn left. *You are back on the Chester to Cardiff road.* Walk as far as the next lane on your left. *Here we leave Ogilby's road but you will walk another section later. The lane, if followed northeast, now joins the A5. A section of the old road has been destroyed by the construction of a canal, a railway and Telford's turnpike (A5). It originally passed through the village of Pentre on its way to cross the River Dee at Newbridge but the road between the A5 and Pentre is now just a footpath.*

Sawmill Cottage

CEFN-WERN
Turn left and along the narrow lane towards Cefn-Wern House. *Pause by the entrance gates and look into the nicely laid gardens. If you are lucky you may see the deer that are free to roam the gardens. The house is also mentioned on Ogilby's map as the residence of Sir Thomas Middleton of Chirk Castle, who had moved to the house during the restoration of the castle after the Civil War.*

Proceed up the lane to the right bend past the rear of the house. *The wooded area on your left was an old quarry which supplied the stone for Cefn-Wern House.* Continue uphill as far as the left bend near the top of the hill. *Stop here for a moment. Look back towards the area on the far side of the valley. Running parallel to the canal and the railway is Telford's turnpike which is now the A5. High on the ridge above there is a much older road and this is outlined against the sky by a very long hedge. This was a military Roman road. It forded the River Dee to the*

79

east of Pentre and goes to the Roman fort that was found by aerial photography at Rhyn Park, which is on the high plateau on the south side of the River Ceiriog.

Look half-left and in the distance you can see Lindisfarne College formerly Wynnstay Hall, the centre of a large estate. It has recently been sold and will be turned into self-contained flats. Beyond the far ridge are the plains of Cheshire, Staffordshire, and further southeast the Wrekin Hills of Shropshire.

OFFA`S DYKE

Continue along the lane and over the brow. *Look half-left and down to the remains of Offa's Dyke, built in the 8th century by King Offa of Mercia on his border with Powys. The enormous earthwork consisting of a ditch 2 metres deep, and on an embankment 2.5 metres high, the whole 130 kilometres long, was probably constructed in only a few weeks.* Carry on down the lane through a wooded area which covers quite a large old marsh. When the lane comes to a small cross roads turn left Continue along the lane as far as the right bend by Fron Cottage. *Here if you look at the hedge immediately in line with the lane that you have just walked there is a different type of hedge planted. This is where an old lane went through. It left the Chester to Cardiff Road and came through Newhall Farm. On Ogilby`s map it is shown as `to ye hills`.*

Proceed uphill along the lane to where it meets with an upper road. *Pause here a moment for, in good weather, you now can see further across Staffordshire and Shropshire to the east.* Turn left and walk as far as the next farm on your left and a footpath marker opposite. Turn right, walk 12 metres and cross the stile into the field on the left. Walk across two fields and cross the stile onto the Pont Fadog Lane. Turn right, and continue along the lane. *When you are by the farm on your right, look half-left and you will get a good view of Chirk Castle.*

TY`N-Y-GROES

When you reach the sharp right bend by Ty'n-y-groes there is a permissive footpath through the castle grounds back to the station. This path is only open between the 26th March to 28th September. Cross the stile to the right side of Ty'n-y-groes Cottage and continue uphill. *You are now on Offa's Dyke Path. The boundary to your left was a quarry road.* Go over the brow and downhill to cross the stile onto a narrow lane.

Turn left and walk down the very narrow worn track . *You are now on the old Oswestry to Llangollen medieval road shown on John Ogilby's Map of 1675. We shall use this road to cross the valley.* Proceed downhill along the old road as far as the modern Ceiriog road, the B4500. **Beware of the traffic** and cross to the lane opposite. *The house on your right was the mill to the castle. The road on this side of the river was not open in Ogilby's time, it was built in 1862.* Continue over the River Ceiriog Bridge and where the road bends left look over the parapet on the right side. *There you will see the old medieval track down to the river where there would have been a ford. The modern bridge has replaced it.*

Carry on uphill and, when the lane meets another, turn left. *When you reach another track, on your right, that is parallel to the road that you are on, stop for a moment. Now, look back across the valley to the dip in the hills opposite the castle mill. This is where Offa's Dyke comes down and you will also notice that the ground on that side is not as steep as the old road that you walked down.* Proceed along the lane. *Look to the track on the right. This was a medieval road from Oswestry to Llangollen shown on Ogilby's map and it can be seen going across the fields parallel and higher than the present road. Eventually the modern road and medieval road join by the old school house further along.*

Continue along the lane and go down the first lane on your left. *You are now back on the Chester/Cardiff road which goes downhill quite steeply and levels alongside the River Ceiriog where it meets the Weston Rhyn road by the Pont Faen Bridge. The bridge is also mentioned on John Ogilby's map. The road from `Pont Vaine` towards `Chirck` on Ogilby's map was closed in the Quarter sessions of 1864, two years after the Chirk to Glyn road was built.*

Turn right and walk uphill then turn left into the lane that is signed for access only. You go past Yew Tree Cottages on your left. When have just passed a wooden cattle shed take the next left turn along a grass track. *This was the original route of the Glyn Valley Tramway. The tramway originally had horsedrawn wagons. It ran to the canal a mile south of*

81

Chirk Bank but was altered when the railway was built. At the end of the woodland track cross the stile into the field and follow the waymarkers.

The Aqueduct, Railway Bridge and Tunnel Entrance

OAKLANDS HALL
After crossing the railway, the canal can be seen on the left below you. When you are level with the yellow brick house on your right go half-right. *This house is Oaklands Hall and is a tower house of two different periods. The open topped tower is part of the original house. The slate roofed tower is part of a later addition. In the trees by the house is the remains of a Norman Motte.* Cross the two stiles either side of the old driveway to the former stables of Oaklands Hall.

COACH ROAD
Continue down a sunken medieval road to a kissing gate. *This exits onto the old 1776 Wrexham to Oswestry coach road.* Turn left. Walk downhill along the pavement. *Above the bridge was a pub, the first this side of the border, but when Telford opened the new toll road below so as not to exceed a gradient of 1 in 22 the publican moved his business to a new pub beside the new road, where it can still be found by the thirsty traveller.*

Go over the canal bridge. *On the far side of the Ceiriog Valley and to the right of the main road there was another motte and bailey. It is now just a hump below a wall. The original Castell-y-waun, guarded the other side of the river. One of these mottes was, no doubt, 'Peverals Tower' said to be 'on the waters of the Ceiriog' in the reign of Henry I (1100-1135).*

ROUTE B Omit the next two paragraphs.

ROUTE A
Turn left along the canal towpath. Carry on alongside the canal as far as the aqueduct. *The canal was opened through Chirk in 1802 constructed by William Jessop. Thomas Telford was the General Agent, Surveyor, Engineer, Architect and Overlooker of the Works. The aqueduct was started in 1796 and it took five years to complete. Henry Robertson later dwarfed the aqueduct with his viaduct built for the Great Western Railway which is 30 metres above the river and was opened in 1848.*

Continue to the canal tunnel. *The 420 metre tunnel, completed in 1802, was mined through solid rock. Be warned, the tunnel is dark in the middle section but there is a handrail to guide you all the way through. Keep dogs on a lead for they are liable to walk off the path.* When you leave the tunnel go twenty metres and turn sharp right up the track. This will take you on to the road above. Turn left and return to Chirk Station.

ROUTE B
Proceed across the coach road to the pavement and continue downhill. At the foot of the hill cross the main road and the bridge. *This was built by Telford in 1831.* Then turn half-right along a footpath which goes past the old Chirk Mill, now an antiques warehouse. Cross the stile and walk over the massive mill leat. Climb the hill on the opposite side as far as the last stile which leads on to the pavement alongside the road. Turn right and walk through the busy village of Chirk as far as the Hand Inn on your right. Turn left into Station Avenue which is opposite the inn, and proceed to the station further along the avenue.

THE END

ROUTE MAP A
Not to scale

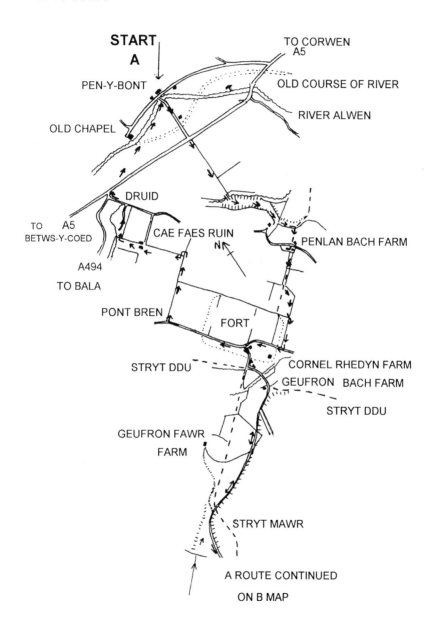

START
A

PEN-Y-BONT

TO CORWEN
A5

OLD COURSE OF RIVER

RIVER ALWEN

OLD CHAPEL

DRUID

TO   A5
BETWS-Y-COED

CAE FAES RUIN

N

PENLAN BACH FARM

A494

TO BALA

PONT BREN

FORT

STRYT DDU

CORNEL RHEDYN FARM

GEUFRON BACH FARM

STRYT DDU

GEUFRON FAWR
FARM

STRYT MAWR

A ROUTE CONTINUED
ON B MAP

A Roman, a Medieval and a Coach Road
CORWEN

START
Route A Pen-y-Bont Lane   SJ052436
Route B Gaerwen   SJ020413

ROUTE A   8 miles (13 kms)
The long walk covers part of a Roman Road, goes through a fort and follows the road to a viewpoint. It returns on a medieval road and finally looks at the old coach road.

ROUTE B   3 miles (5kms)
The shorter walk covers part of a Roman military road which runs between Penrhos fort and Brithdir. It starts at a viewpoint.

HOW TO GET THERE
Route A   By Bus There is a daily bus service from Corwen to Druid. Alight from the bus at Cefn Rug Farm, walk west towards Druid and the first lane on your right is Pen-y-bont Lane.

By Car Leave Corwen and go along the A5 for two miles towards Druid. Carry on through the traffic lights at the junction of the A494 (T). Take the first left (Pen-y-bont Lane). Fork first left ignoring the lane to Bettws Gwerful-Goch. Go past a cottage on the left and round a left bend and continue past the cottages on the right. A footbridge across the river can be seen on the left. Vehicles can be parked on the road verge prior or past the bridge.

Route B By Car only From Corwen take the B440I to Cynwyd and then turn right in the village to the River Dee bridge. Follow the lane until a staggered cross roads, turn right and then left. Where the lane bends right take the No Through Road on the left. Continue uphill to the end of the surfaced lanc on the ridge of the hill. There are spaces on the verge to park a vehicle.

HISTORY

Two thousand miles or more of Roman roads are to be found in Wales, nearly all completed during the first century of Roman occupation. It is apparent that there are many gaps in our knowledge of the road system. Some known ones appear to end abruptly for no obvious reason. Others have large missing portions but continue after perhaps a mile or two at some distant place, maybe on a different alignment. It may be possible to spot the changes in direction of a road from fords or at hilltops.

The large fort which lies northwest of Corwen protects at least eight Roman roads which enter the Vale. All have large gaps and no one can say for certain where they are coming from or going to, except for three which have been traced through to their destinations. The first road runs between Wroxeter (Uriconio) and Kanovium (Caerhun). The second road runs between Chester (Deva) and Brithdir. A third road goes to Ruthin, Denbigh and St Asaph. Perhaps sometime in the future the destinations of the other roads will be found.

We know all about the Norman invasion of Britain. It took nearly another two hundred years or so before they were finally established in Wales. Like the Romans they needed to police the area so wooden castles were built on the top of stone and earth mounds. All that remains of these castle structures are the earth mounds namely the mottes. These take some searching for nowadays, most often they became levelled when land was required. They are now protected.

The Corwen Vale was important in the Roman and Norman periods. Like the axis of a spoked wheel, it was a centre where many roads spread out in different directions going deep into Wales.

The mottes were built on or close to main routes. Sometimes these were the old Roman roads, if they were on the same route to suite the Norman destination, otherwise the Normans would construct new roads using local labour.

These Norman roads were more like tracks, no more than three metres wide. The surface was flat with a light scatter of stones. if the road was along the side of a valley, a kerb would be constructed along the outer side. This was to stop small carts going off the track

86

Many of the tracks can still be found today if the whereabouts of mottes are known e.g. the Rug Estate Motte and the Tomen-y-castell Motte near Llanfor on the Bala A494 road. The medieval tracks are still intact in places and specially if they have been reused by farms. These roads were lower in the valleys on arable land and this is one of the reasons why they were destroyed more often than the Roman roads which usually had been built on high ground only suitable for grazing.

The main difference between the Roman and the Norman roads was the road surface. The Roman road was usually wider and had a raised cambered stony surface. These roads only turned before or after fords or on a brow of a hill The Roman fords would have a raised causeway.

The footbridge over the Alwen replaces an earlier road upstream

DIRECTIONS

ROUTE B Go to the bottom of page 90

ROUTE A Go over the River Alwen footbridge and along the lane until you reach the A5. Opposite, use the concrete stile and walk alongside the hedge on your left. Cross the small concrete footbridge and continue straight on keeping a large pheasant pen on your right. The path enters a shallow hollow and goes half-left onto a terraced path. Where this path goes downhill fork half-right and take the path which climbs uphill. Continue past some bushes on your left, and follow a wire fence on your left. Cross the stile by boulders. After 50 metres take steps in a dip to your right (their poor condition reported to the council) and climb into the field above. Head for the fieldgate onto the lane by Penlan Bach Farm.

PENLAN BACH FARM

Proceed through the farm entrance gate (please shut it after you). Look directly ahead, there are some steps between two barns. This is the way of the path. Turn left behind the barns and go to a wire fence on the right (there should be a stile) which goes across an old track. Climb over the fence onto the track and carry on uphill. *This is a Roman road which entered the fort at the top of the hill. A lot of water has flowed down the old road and it is surprising just how much of it still survives. Running down the centre of the older road there is a track of about two metres wide. This has been caused by later farm carts cutting through the Roman surface. At the top of the old road there has been a very large pool (on the left). This was a reservoir for the farm below. Take note of the stones that have been used to construct the pool sides and the dam, a lot of them are shaped and it is possible that these may have come from the Roman fort which may have had some stone buildings inside a wooden fortification.*

PENRHOS ROMAN FORT

Proceed uphill, and on reaching the crest the road disappears due to ploughing. The footpath follows the hedge on your left. As the hedge bends further away to the left, continue straight across the field to the gate in the far corner. *From where the road vanished there is evidence of a very slight ridge which runs in the centre of the field, under a crossing hedge, and goes downhill towards Four Crosses Lane. This ridge is all that remains of the Roman fort southeast defence embankment. A fort seen from aerial photographs lies on the southwest side of hill. The northwest corner is just below the present lane at MR 0089/4260. The northeast corner is at MR 0410/4290 The southeast corner at MR 0413/4280. Cornel-Rhedyn Farm lies in the southwest corner of the fort. Therefore the total area of the fort is quite substantial*

Go through the field gate and continue with the hedge on your right until reaching the Four Crosses Lane. Turn right up this lane. *It goes through the grounds of the old fort. The ridge previously mentioned is now a hollow between the footpath exit and the next field gate on the right. A section of hedge has been implanted across this hollow. Opposite there is a field gate and quite a large ditch running down the right side of the field. This is the remains of the southern defensive ditch. The building to the right of this ditch is part of Cornel-Rhedyn Farm.*

GEUFRON BACH

Continue along the lane round a left bend and a right bend until reaching another cottage on the left. Turn left down the narrow lane just beyond. *Stop at the end of the first straight and where the lane bends left. You are now standing at what was a Roman cross roads. Opposite the left turn in the lane there is a field gate and in a low sun an old track can be seen running northwest across the field. This is a Roman road called Stryt Ddu. It runs between Conwy (Konovium) and Wroxeter (Uriconio). Directly ahead is a field access. The lower section of the lane that you walked down was the original entrance into the fort. Its continuation, which is now the field access, originally went straight across the fields and up the slope to the left of the Geufron Fawr Farm hill access track This old road went to Llanfor near Bala. You will see it when you get further up the hill.*

Continue around the left bend along the lane. The lane goes slightly uphill and then descends into a wet hollow. Here the lane has been built up over a piped stream. Carry on around the rear of Geufron Bach Farm. *Look at the fields either side of the lane here, they were probably marshes in the Roman period, and an aid in the fort's defences.*

89

GEUFRON BACH FARM

Walk along the track which leaves the rear of the Geufron Bach farmhouse and starts to climb the side of the hill. Ignore a track going up to the left. *The old road here has been widened for the use of farm vehicles. Look to the right side of this road and in places you will see a second hedge which is lower than the one alongside the road. This hedge was on an earlier estate road. Material has been pulled down from the left side to make the track much wider for farm vehicles.*

900 metres above the farm you approach a slight left bend in the road.

ROUTE B RETURNS UPHILL FROM HERE
ROUTE A CONTINUES UPHILL

The public path is uphill on the main track. *Look below the main track and you will see the access track from Geufron Fawr, which is a deep rutted tree-lined hollow in the hillside. Look to the immediate right of this and close to the fence. There is another hollow which is separate from the access track. Above the main track, to your left is another deep hollow going uphill, soil has been dumped in the lower part. This deep hollow is the remains of the Roman road. I am sure that the landowner would not mind if you walked up it, as it negotiates the hillside far more easily than the later farm track Two thirds of the way up you have no option but to follow this main track as the Roman road goes on the opposite side of the fence going uphill to the top of the ridge, where it rejoins the later road. When you reach the top the hedge on your left is a parish boundary. It is not unusual to find a parish boundary along a Roman road.*

Continue until you reach the council lane on your left.

ROUTE B STARTS HERE. Go through the gate and turn left.
THE RIDGEWAY

This is the highest part of the walk and the views over the hills can only be described as wonderful, especially on a clear day. To the northeast and high above Corwen is the hillfort Caer Drewyn, the only hillfort in Wales where the defence wall can be seen from seven miles away The Dee Valley lies to the southeast and the Glan-yr-Afon Valley to the northwest. The latter is where all the main routes ran through to Bala. The two

ROUTE MAP B
Not to scale

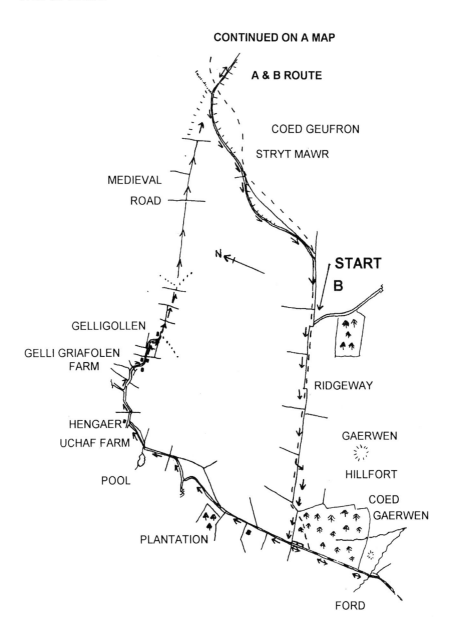

CONTINUED ON A MAP

A & B ROUTE

COED GEUFRON

STRYT MAWR

MEDIEVAL
ROAD

N

START
B

GELLIGOLLEN

GELLI GRIAFOLEN
FARM

RIDGEWAY

HENGAER
UCHAF FARM

GAERWEN

HILLFORT

POOL

COED
GAERWEN

PLANTATION

FORD

valleys are used by low flying aircraft and it is not unusual to find yourself looking down into a cockpit of a passing jet. To the southwest there is a high point and just below this is the remains of the settlement Gaerwen (this is on private land), which dates from the Iron Age earlier than the hillfort Caer Drewyn.

THE ROMAN ROAD

Go through a gate. *On your left look for a dog-leg in the wall. Stand by this and look back along the wall and you will see half of the width of the Roman road. The other half is on the footpath side and has been destroyed, although there are marks in the ground showing where it had been. The full width of the road would have been 8 metres.*

Continue along the path and go through two more gates. Look for a gate on the left. The bridleway from here is waymarked. Go through the gate.

Roman Road

Turn half right and follow the track across the field. You will pass a small outcrop of rocks on your right, from here the track descends a little and runs to a pinewood enclosed by a wall on your left. Carry on along the track by this wall. *Look for a large gap where the wall has fallen away. Now look left and slightly below the wall foundation where you will see the remains of a sunken track. This is the Roman road. There is no point in trying to follow it through the woods because most of it has been destroyed. Later on I will tell you where it exits from the wood.*

THE FORD
Resume downhill and go across a marshy area. Exit the marsh onto a crossing track. Turn left through the gate and go downhill. *Beyond the sheep pens on your left look for a track which comes out of the woods. This was the Roman road, it has been reused for a forest road. Take note now of how the remainder of the track ahead of you changes. It is wider and there is a cambered shape to the old surface, in places this has been cut through by iron wheeled farm carts and the road stones can be seen.*

Return from the ford

93

Continue downhill leaving the woods until you reach the ford. *Now look left and you will see what looks like an outcrop of rocks from the surrounding marsh. I have been here one very dry summer. Its shape could be described as a small camp, possibly to guard the ford which was an important road junction in Roman times. The road or track that you can see going uphill and bending to the right goes to Llanfor (Bala). A second road or track going to the left, goes across the Dee Valley and over the Berwyns to Llansilin forming part of the Roman network*

THE RETURN
Turn back the way you came along the road and go through the gate. Do not turn right but continue straight through another gate and below an animal shelter. Go up a slight rise keeping a wall on the right and the forestry plantation on your left. The worn stony track is easy to follow as it now descends downhill. It does a little zigzag which makes it easier for walkers. On the last right bend the track rejoins the wall on the right, turns left and goes straight down for a considerable distance. Go through the gate. *Before going downhill look to the right to see the shelf of an earlier track which has been partly destroyed by the later ditch. This is an early medieval road which replaced the Roman road on the top of the hills.* Turn right down a steep descent.

HENGAER UCHAF
Proceed downhill and go through another gate to enter Hengaer Ucha Farm. At the farmhouse turn right along the driveway. Continue along the lane downhill

GELLI-GRIAFOLEN
Ignore the lane to the left and carry on to Gelli-Griafolen Farm. Go through the farm gate and follow the road into the farmyard which then bends left to pass between two barns. Continue along the lane through two gates. Ignore the field gate on the left but stay with the lane as it climbs quite steeply uphill bending to the right and then to the left around to the rear of Gelli-Gollen .

GELLI-GOLLEN
Follow the road until it bends right to a small garage. The footpath is to the left of the garage and two low strands of barbed wire hang across a

gap in the rear hedge. (There should, of course, be a stile) Go into the field. *Stop, you are now on the medieval road. Look right: although covered in shrubs and very overgrown this is part of the road. In the fields beyond it has been obliterated Remember the section near to Hen gaer. it is part of this is old road. Short sections can be found in-between on private land. The right of way goes to the Ridgeway.*

THE MEDIEVAL ROAD

Turn left. *The road you are about to walk is very narrow and is over 700 years old. It probably was a main medieval road which connected the early Norman Mottes at Rug Estate and at Tomen-y-castell (Llanfor).*
Keep the hedge and fence on your left as the path climbs uphill. *The road along this section is very eroded and much of it looks like the natural slope of the hill.*

At a wooden fence continue into the next field. Here the terrace of the road can be seen as it follows the natural curve of the hill on an even level. Go through the wall gap then con the green road, keeping a scrappy hedge on the left side. The ground rises sharply on the right side.

At the end of the hedge a later track cuts across the road. Be careful not to follow this other track downhill or the track uphill. During the summer the route of the old road straight ahead on the level is hidden by tall ferns. Where the later track goes across the medieval road look for a small tree on the right alongside the road. *It may have been noticed that although the road is level the valley is now lower. Where there are gaps on the left in the trees, you will realise just how high the road is from the valley floor. If this road had been Roman, the wooded valley side would have been an ideal place for an ambush. Instead of making narrow tracks along the sides of valleys, the Romans preferred wider roads across the hilltop moors where they could march in force, and be in less fear of an ambush.*

Carry on along the terrace until entering a wooded area where the route is easier to follow. *A slight bend left and right has been caused by a spring on the right just above the road. Wet earth has been pushed down onto the original road surface and later travellers have negotiated around this causing the road to bend a little.*

Go along the road, avoiding fallen trees and across a fence, until it breaks out of the wood. Here is an old stone gate post. *Over the next short section the ground has been disturbed removing any evidence of the trail.* Continue to follow the curve of the slope towards the fence on the right. *This is where the medieval road originally joined the Geufron Bach track.*

The footpath joins the Geufron Bach track at an old gateway. *Take note of the very large boulder at the top of Geufron Fawr track. It may have been a boundary stone. One side has been shaped. There may have been letters on this section but time has eroded them away.*

ROUTE A Turn left.
ROUTE B Turn right. Go to the second paragraph of page 90.

PONT BREN
Continue downhill past the farm and return along the lane. Around the bend at the T-junction turn left and walk along until you reach Pont Bren, the first house on the left. Go through the gate opposite. Proceed through two fields (no stile was in place at the time of writing.) keeping a wire fence on your left.

CAEFAES
Go through the gate in the left corner. In twenty metres take the gate on your left and turn right. Walk downhill along an old farm entrance track. Keep the ruins of Caefaes Farm on your right. At the end of the barn turn half-right and go across the rear of the old farmhouse. At the rear of the house the ground falls quite steeply. Walk with care down this slope until you reach the bank of the stream. Turn right and go to a wire fence, there is a gap in the wire. (There should, of course, be a stile here.) Continue along the path on the bank of the stream.

DRUID
When the stream runs to the left, stay straight on, until you find a stone track which takes you through the tiny village of Druid. *Although the old houses have been refurbished it is quite easy to see which was the mill, another a large barn, and the miller's cottage.* Follow the track until it meets with a lane.

THE COACH ROAD

Turn left. *Look for the first wooden field gate on your left. The field beyond the gate is long and very narrow and it was once the Bala coach road (1776). At the upper end of the field the modern A494 (T) bends around cutting through the coach road. The field on the far side of the modern road is known as Cae Sarn (Paved Field). It refers to the coach road and not a Roman road.*

Go along the lane to its junction with the A494. Go onto the right-hand path of the main road to the traffic lights on the A5 Beware of fast cars from the right, and cross the A5 to a field gate and footpath sign. Walk diagonally right across the field and continue alongside the River Alwen.

The course of the river was changed when Telford built the A5 turnpike road; the old course of the river can be seen to your right. The large stone embankment alongside the river was built during the construction of the turnpike to prevent the river from flooding the low fields and the new road.

At the end of the field use the concrete stile. Turn left onto the lane and cross the footbridge.

Bewick Woodcut

97

ROUTE MAP
Not to scale

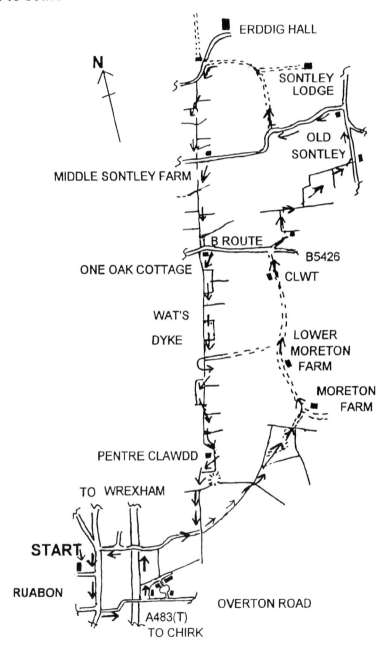

A Medieval Supply Road
RUABON

START
Library Car Park

ROUTE A   6 Miles (10 kms)
From Ruabon to Erddig is fairly flat with views towards the Welsh hills.

ROUTE B   3 Miles (5 kms)
You can decide whether to take this shortcut after a mile or so.

HOW TO GET THERE
By Train
Ruabon is on the Wrexham/Shrewsbury line.
By Bus
The Wrexham/Cefn and Wrexham/ Llangollen buses pass through the village.
By Car
The village of Ruabon can be found on the old Wrexham to Chirk road. The library car park is the first turning on the right past the shops, coming from the Wrexham direction **or**: from the bypass (A483) take the turn off signposted Ruabon. In the village take the turning for the library and car park which is between the church and the shops.

DIRECTIONS
Leave the car park and go to the main street. Turn right along the pavement until you reach the church. Cross the road to the Wynnstay Hotel then turn left onto the Overton road. Keep on the left pavement and stop for a moment at the left bend. *Directly ahead of you are the old entrance gates to Wynnstay Park. They will never to be used again because the new bypass has cut them off from the old driveway to the Park.*

Continue along the pavement and cross the bypass bridge. Turn left immediately at the end of the bridge onto a footpath. Walk along this, parallel to the bypass until you reach the field ahead. *Stop by the stile for a moment. If you look to your right you will see a hedge which stands away from the rear boundary of some properties. This was a footpath and originally an old road. The path has been closed off. This is a branch of an old road of medieval origin which linked two mottes (Norman castles.) The main line of the old road which you will join later was traced to a motte which stands alongside the A5 close to the village of Pentre.*

The road originally went south to James's Farm, which lies halfway between the western boundary of Wynnstay Park and the Ruabon/Cefn-mawr road. At the farm it joined an old Roman road which went south to a ford on the River Dee just below Pentre. It then ran through the village to the motte. Soon you will walk some of the road which goes north to the motte by Erddig Park.

Cross the stile ahead and proceed to the next stile by the bridge over the bypass. Turn right and climb the hill ahead. *The track here was made for farm vehicle access, but if you look to your right beyond the old quarry, you will see the original track which is no more that two metres wide, it joins the medieval motte road at Moreton Farm. Originally this track, a branch from the main medieval road, went to the Gardden Hillfort on the northwest side of Ruabon. The actual route through the town has been destroyed but if you look back from the brow of the hill you will have an aerial view of its original course.*

The path comes to a junction; you are now on Wat's Dyke. Turn half left and climb the stile ahead. Walk beside the hedge on your right and take the next stile. Keep alongside the hedge which is now on your left. *Halfway along look over this hedge and you will see a hollow parallel to the path, this is the course of the branch medieval road.*

MORTON-ANGLICORUM
Climb the next stile and go half-right. *As you walk across this field you will cross a hollow which goes from your left to your right, it goes in a large arc towards a lane and your next stile. This hollow is the branch of the old road.*

100

Continue to the stile and onto the existing lane. Proceed through the field gate at the rear of Moreton Farm. *You are now on the medieval road which also served a. fifteenth century township which was on the fields to the south. The village was called Morton-Anglicorum and it was probably destroyed during the period when the black death was rampant in England. Whole villages were put to the torch during this period to eradicate the disease. Nowadays the remains of the village can only be seen on aerial photographs.*

Go to your left of the building ahead and continue along the track. The next farm that you pass on your right is Lower Moreton Farm. Carry on along this track. *The farm on your left is Clwt (the patch.) Once part of the Newhall Estate, the farmhouse was built on the site of former stables.* Continue until you reach the B5426.

ROUTE B (Shortcut)
Turn left, proceed around the left bend and take the stile on your left, before One Oak Cottage. **Go to page 103**

ROUTE A continued
Cross the road to the access track opposite. Directly ahead is the ruin of a cottage, the stile is to your left of this ruin.*The road across the field has been completely obliterated by the plough.* Continue directly ahead to cross the stile in the next hedge. Turn right. *You are now leaving the route of the old road but we shall rejoin it later.*

Proceed along the path with the hedge on your right, climb the next stile and go half-left across the field. Go through a gate and walk ten metres to pass through a gate on your right, resume walking along the hedge on your left to the next field gate. Turn left and, beyond the gate, descend sharply onto a field access track and a gate on the right which will bring you out onto Sontley Lane by Old Sontley Farm. *Once owned by the Norman ' Sonlli' family, this medieval hall is now split into two farms.*

ERDDIG
Turn left and walk along Sontley Lane. You will pass the old mill cottage on your right. When you reach two semi-detached cottages turn left along the lane and continue to the sharp bend left. Turn right onto the track. *This is the continuation of the medieval road. At a large pond on your*

right there is an old drive which goes to Sontley Lodge Farm. This drive went out of use when the Sontley Lane was constructed.

ERDDIG HALL

Continue ahead along the medieval road as it bends left towards the present entrance drive to Erddig Hall. Go through the kissing gate on your right. *Look to the rear of the small cottage. Here you will see a hollow which comes out of the cottage garden and goes down the embankment to your right. This is the remains of the medieval road. The cottage has been built on top of the road. The road then continues below this embankment until it reaches the motte on the far side of Erddig Hall. A later road, constructed by the first owners of Erddig Hall, goes to Wrexham and has destroyed the latter section of the medieval road.* If you require refreshments, there is a shop and cafe in the courtyard of the hall, which is situated to your right at the end of this entrance drive. National Trust members can enter the house free, others must pay.

The house, built by Joshua Edisbury in the late 17th century, still forms the central part of Erddig. Thomas Webb of Middlewich added wings in the 1720s and Wyatt stone-faced the west front in the 1770s. Erddig was no architectural masterpiece but owes its enrichment in the early eighteenth century to John Meller, a prosperous London lawyer involved in Joshua Edisbury's bankruptcy case, who bought the house. He bequeathed the estate, in 1733, to his nephew Simon Yorke, the first of a direct line of Simon and Phillip Yorkes who were owners of Erddig until 1973, when the last Squire, Phillip Yorke III, gave the property and 1,942 acres to the National Trust.

RETURN ALONG WAT'S DYKE

From the cattle grid by the cottage go left along the drive heading away from the hall. At the first right bend there is an iron stile on your left. The footpath along the dyke towards Middle Sontley Farm has been waymarked by the National Trust and you should not get lost here. There *is very little known about the border dykes despite over 100 excavations on them. Wat's Dyke is assumed to have been constructed at around the time of Offa's Dyke or probably slightly later. Ditches and banks were a common Saxon defence around villages but the idea of using one to partition a country may have come from Hadrian's Roman vallum (ditch) across the Scottish border. The medieval road that you have been*

102

following may date to the same period or earlier and may have been a border supply road.

When you reach the farm on Sontley Lane turn left. Do not take the first track as this only goes to the fishing pools, but turn right onto the track with the footpath sign. The path along this section of the dyke is straight and clearly waymarked until you reach the B5426. *The footpath on your right at the first stile is another hollow way worth looking at. It was originally another branch from the medieval road although most of it to your left have been wiped out. If you wander down to take a look return here to continue ahead to the B5426.* At this road beware of the traffic. Cross the stile opposite, alongside One Oak Cottage.

ROUTE B joins here
From the rear of the cottage go half-right. There is a waymarker post indicating the route onto the top of the dyke. *As you walk the dyke, take note of the fields on your left, they all have large butts and reins (ridge and furrows), indicating that this land had once been very wet.* After leaving the enclosed dyke cross the small bridge ahead and follow the deep ditch on your right. The dyke itself has been ploughed down almost level across the next three fields except for another short section that you walk along.. At a crossing farm track, climb the stile opposite (hidden behind the gate) and continue to follow the dyke hedge on your right.

At the end of this field cross the stile on your right, the path continues to the left between a field hedge and the dyke until the next stile ahead. One more stile and the path goes uphill towards Pentre-Clawdd (village-on-the-dyke) Farm alongside the fence on the right. Keep left around the buildings. Go through the yard gates and keep the old quarry on your left.

JOURNEY'S END
At the first bend of the farm lane take the gate on your left. Follow the hedge (on the dyke) ahead until you reach the stile in the corner of the field that you initially came over. Retrace your steps down the track until you reach the bridge over the bypass. Go over this and past Ruabon School. At the shops, cross the main road and turn left along the pavement. The next road on your right goes to the library car park.

THE END

ROUTE MAP
Not to scale

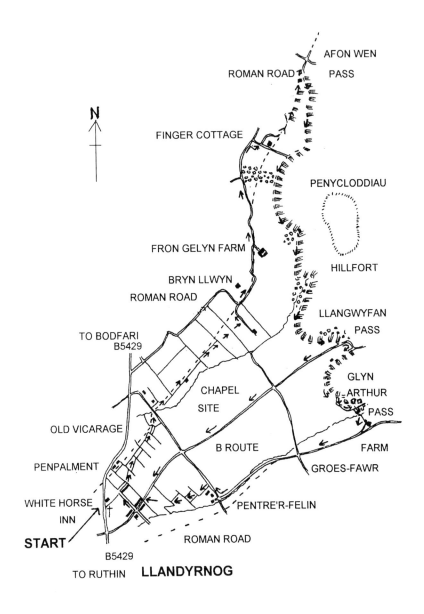

Roman Passes
LLANDYRNOG (NORTHEAST)

START
The White Horse Inn   SJ107652

ROUTE A   8 miles (12 kms) Ascent 825m
The walk takes you on a Roman road to the Afon Wen Pass along an estate road which is now a bridleway, giving you a pleasant walk and breathtaking views high above the Vale of Clwyd. Return along the Glyn Arthur Pass Roman road and across green pastures that once belonged to one of the great estates, back to the village.

ROUTE B 7 Miles (10 kms) Ascent 825m
The short route is just a quick escape route straight down the road from the Llangwyfan Pass in case of bad weather.

HOW TO GET THERE
By Bus
A service which runs through the village between Denbigh and Ruthin.

By Car
Parking is available at The White Horse Inn in the village, **by request**.

   From Denbigh Leave on the A525 at the first roundabout. Turn left at the second road, signposted Llandyrnog 3 miles. At the next roundabout turn right and continue round a right bend and a left bend. The White Horse Inn is on the left.
   From Ruthin Follow the A494 Mold road for two miles to the village of Llanbedr-Dyffryn-Clwyd. Turn left at the village church signposted Llandyrnog 5 miles. On entering the village the White Horse Inn is on the right next to the church.
   From Mold Depart on the A541 Denbigh road. In 12 miles take the B5429 left turn, signposted Llandyrnog 3 miles. On entering the village the White Horse Inn is on the left next to the church.

HISTORY

The footpaths that you are about to walk have a history which goes back some eighteen hundred years. These paths were in use as roads and tracks up to the early seventeenth century. Any part of these ancient roads which did not fit into the later systems, was ploughed out leaving only a public right of way across the fields. As you are no doubt aware, footpaths have been moved since the early estates took over large tracts of land. This gives the historian some problems in finding the exact route of a Roman road.

The walk introduces you to a section of a Roman road that did not go out of use until the late nineteenth century. Part of it is still in use today. The road branched off the Denbigh to Ruthin Roman road in the village of Pentre Llanrhaeadr which is on the west side of the Vale of Clwyd. It forded the Rivers Clwyedog and Clwyd to go through Llandyrnog on its way to the Afon Wen Pass in the hills to the northeast, where it continued to Caerwys.

DIRECTIONS ROUTE A & B

From the rear of the White Horse Inn go straight along the footpath which is opposite the cobbled passage between the inn and the church. Continue behind the council houses' gardens until you reach a stile into a field. Go half-left to a stile by a field gate on the opposite side of the field heading towards the Creamery chimney. Continue directly ahead until the next stile which leads onto a field access track.

PENPALMENT

Stop here for a moment and look back at the white farmhouse which was on your left when you crossed the last field. The farm is named Penpalment, in English it means top or end pavement. It is not referring to the pavement on the side of the B5429. It refers to a Roman road. When the Romans made their roads the surface was paved. This does not necessarily mean large slabs, it could also refer to small stones embedded into a hard material. In places there are roads where the stones have just been thrown down. It all depends on what type of ground the road is to pass over. Whenever there is a name like this, there is usually a Roman road.

106

The road originally passed close to the farmhouse. If you look at the hedge near the end of the house there is a gate, this is where the road came through. It then crossed the field below where you are standing and went along the rear boundary of the milk bottling factory. In the past when this field was ploughed there was a long row of stones across the turned ground indicating the route of the road. The right of way has been removed from the old road and replaced where you are standing.

Resume the walk along the field access to the next field gate. Directly ahead is another stile and the path is between a fence and a hedge. The path is somewhat neglected as the result of recent cut-backs in the local Authority budget, for up to this year the path was regularly cleared. At the end of the enclosed path, step over another stile and turn half-left to the lane.

If you look back now you will notice that you are on high ground. This is where the Roman road was heading and for a particular reason. Roman roads only make a turn (re-alignments) on brows of hills or at fords. The Romans purposely constructed the road to this hill to make the re-alignment. If the road had been laid through the fields on the north side, it would have run into marshy ground. In the middle of the field you will see a hollow going downhill to a stream. This was the realigned Roman road and, incidentally, it later became part of the old parish boundary here. The road forded the stream and then re-aligned again to follow the course of the stream to the right.

Take the stile opposite, into a field. Turn half-left and step across the stream, turn right and continue up the slope. *You are now on the Roman road. The large house on your left was the vicarage. The lane that you crossed was a medieval road which ran between Rhuddlan Castle and the Shropshire markets.*

CHAPEL SITE
Go straight ahead through the gateway and continue up the field keeping the hedge on your right. *Take note of the unusual amount of stones along the hedge bottoms. Actually along this section the road stones are still in place, but they are 600mm below the surface.* Continue over the next stile and follow the path still keeping the hedge on your right.

Keep your eyes open along here because in the hedge halfway up this large field you will see iron railings. Behind them there is a slate slab with Welsh writing on it. Behind the slab is the original stone. The inscription records that this was the site of the first Methodist Chapel allowed in Llandyrnog during 1749. In those days the church owned most of the land in the village.

When the Methodists wanted to build a chapel the parish church would only allow it to be built outside their boundary. As this was the busiest road outside the church boundary at that time, the chapel was first built here. In 1836, when the road fell out of use, it was moved closer to the village.

Roman Road and Bridleway

Resume the walk to the stile at the top of this field. From here the hedge is on your left. *The Roman road is on the opposite side of the hedge. The footpath has been moved away from the route of the road, although we shall see the road again shortly.*

After the next stile the hedge has been removed. *Look for a natural spring welling up out of the ground a few metres ahead.* The path goes straight uphill to a stile and hedge directly ahead. *Stop here for a moment, for you will notice that there is a concrete slab path running parallel to the hedge. This path was reinstated by the T B Sanatorium at Llangwyfan, which is in the trees to you right. Each slab is numbered. This was an aid to TB sufferers who walked the path. The nurse in charge would keep a record of the number that the patient could walk to each week. If the number got higher it would show an improvement in the patient's health.*

PEN LLWYN

Go over the stile and continue straight on, up a steeper climb onto a stony track (footpath) where you turn left. *The large building that you could see in the trees to your right when you came up the steep field is Vron Yw House (house on the hillside) originally owning most of the land this side of Llandyrnog.*

The track that you are on bends to the right and straightens out to avoid quite a steep dip in the field. *Stop, turn round and look beyond the bend in the track and just below the shoulder of the dip. There you will see the Roman road coming uphill to join the section of the track that you are standing on.*

Proceed along the straight piece of track until it comes to a gate which exits onto the Pen Llwyn lane. Turn right up the hill. *It is obvious the lane has been modernised up the hill to the entrance to Fron-Gelyn Farm on the right. The views along the vale from here are quite good but not as impressive as the views that you will see on the top road.*

Continue up the lane. *Beyond the entrance to the farm the lane has not been modernised except for a thin surface dressing which occasionally reveals the stones beneath. The left hedge is very young compared to the hedge on the right. The Roman road goes uphill on an easy gradient.*

Follow the road through the right bend. The gradient is quite steep and then levels out once more. *This is typical of Roman construction when going uphill in short steps.*

Follow the lane around a left bend. *Look for a field gate on the right which will be referred to later. This is the way that the Roman road probably went although there is no evidence of any track or terrace going diagonally across the slope. It may have just eroded away through lack of use or possibly have been buried by loose shale that forms the general makeup of the hillside. From the gate and where the Roman road may have been, is the line of an old parish boundary.*

Continue along the modern lane past the dip where another lane joins from the left. The lane bends to the right and bends left and levels once more. Just around the next bend right, you will turn right into another narrow metalled lane. Within twenty metres there is a bridleway on your left. Go through the gate onto a wooded hill and follow the track curving to the right through silver birch trees.

FINGER COTTAGE
The track bends to the right and then descends. *Look directly ahead at the hillside facing you. There is a track which can be seen going uphill from right to left. This is the Roman road and the old parish boundary. On a detailed OS map you would see that the track to the right goes down the hillside to the gate where you stopped earlier.*

Proceed downhill. *Among the trees to the right is Finger Cottage which you will see later.*

At the bottom of the hill bend left and go over a small ford. Follow the bridleway uphill until it levels out. *Here the Roman road joins the bridleway.*

Continue straight on and where the bridleway bends left to go downhill alongside the old parish boundary, there is a gate directly ahead. This a footpath and the Roman road. Go thought the gate and follow the Roman road which you can plainly see as a terrace going uphill. Near the top of the terrace, go through another field gate and there is a fence on your left.

Follow the road around a slight right bend to reach the top of the terrace. Just prior to the brow, the fence goes across the road and you have no alternative but to go along the sheep track alongside this fence. On reaching the top and level ground, a bridleway joins from the right. *The Roman road is now on the opposite side of the fence on your left.*

This bridleway will be your route but first continue straight ahead along the bridleway until you reach a field gate and stile on the left but do not go over the stile. *Look directly ahead at the tree-lined track which goes over the shoulder of the hill in front of you. This was the Afon Wen Roman road.*

THE BRIDLEWAY
Return the way you came until you reach the fork of the tracks. Bear left along the top bridleway. *This track was probably an estate road constructed by several of the large estates in the Vale of Clwyd, to provide a much improved access to the Afon Wen pass.*

Continue along the bridleway for 4 kilometres stopping, when you desire, to admire the fine views to the sea in the north and along the vale below. The way bends right and then returns to the left. Ignore the small track on the right which goes straight downhill. *On the right is Finger Cottage in the trees.*

Go on around a left bend. *There is an area on the right of dense prickly gorse. Go past this and look straight down the hillside. This is where the parish boundary goes across the slope to the field gate mentioned previously. Even from the top looking down there is no evidence of any old road across the slope except a dip in the old parish boundary some 80m above the road which was made after the boundary. What you will see is a lot of loose shale just below the fence to the bridleway and it is probably this that has either buried the road or washed it away. High above on the hills on your left is Penycloddiau, the largest hillfort in North Wales, covering 12 hectares. The fort was protected by ditches and embankments, hence the mountain's name (top of the dykes).*

The bridleway continues into a long left bend and returns to a right bend to cross a wooded stream. *Here, a thoughtful farmer has placed a large metal water tank to collect a supply of fresh water which would have been piped to a farm below. The size of this tank is enormous, it must have been carried piece by piece up the hill and assembled here. It is now so old and rusty that the water is pouring out from a hole in its base.*

LLANGWYFAN PASS
The bridleway continues along a good straight section and goes round a sharp bend left, returning round a right bend to cross another wooded mountain stream. Beyond, the track wanders through a wooded section until leaving the trees to another sharp left bend. The way straightens out and goes through a field gate directly ahead. From here it narrows and descends to a sharp left bend. It then continues to descend along a terrace until it joins the modern road of the Llangwyfan Pass.

ROUTE B (shortcut or bad weather escape route)
Turn right downhill. By the village shop turn right to the Inn.

ROUTE A
Turn left and continue around a right bend which takes the road across a stream. Immediately take the bridleway off to the right. This rough track is the continuation of the earlier bridleway. The track snakes uphill and through a field gate where it passes Pen-y-Bryn, an unusual half-built house on the right. *At the top of the climb stop for a moment and look to your right across the valley. There you will see the Llangwyfan Sanatorium at the foot of the hills.*

Continue along the track going around a left bend onto a straight and now you are overlooking the Vale of Clwyd. Walk on until the track starts to bend to the left again. Look for the large wooded area on the right. Cross the rough stile at the start of these woods and descend quite sharply down the hillside through the often overgrown wood keeping a fence on your right. As the fence veers to the left follow the woodland edge and go through the small gate in the next corner. Go down the field keeping the fence on your right. At the foot of the slope turn right through a field gate. *This track was an old drive which went to Glyn Arthur Hall which is further up the valley.* Turn immediately left across the stream.

GALES BACH
Climb diagonally uphill to a stile onto a lane at the entrance to Gales Bach. ***The lane that you now are on was a Roman road which has been***

reused for modern vehicles getting to the houses at the top of the valley. The Roman road originally went through the Glyn Arthur Pass to Cilcain. Turn right downhill. *Where the lane is cut deep and the hedges are quite high either side, you will notice a very narrow shelf along the bottom of the hedge. This was the level of the old Roman road, the lane has been deepened on purpose to lessen the gradient for horsedrawn carts.*

At Groes Fawr (great cross) crossroads, go straight ahead and continue on the narrow lane which descends around a right bend. *As the lane returns to a left bend look very carefully on the left side in the overgrown hedge, you will see a track which leaves the lane. This is the Roman road, it cannot be followed because it goes over private land. It originally joined the Palment road that you walked from Llandyrnog but further west of the village and close to the River Clwyd. At the point where the Roman road leaves it is obvious that the lane that you are now on is of a later period because it swings right and descends quite quickly onto a level which could be easily flooded from a nearby stream. The reason why the Roman road was not re-used from this point is that it did not go near the corn mill which had been built on the stream to the right.*

Continue along the lane for a short distance passing Pentre Felin (village mill) on the right. *On the 1893 First Edition OS map it shows that the lane originally went to the mill and left again downstream. Since then, the mill has been converted to a dwelling house and the lane system has been changed to go around.* At the next cross roads do not go straight across for it is a private lane to a farm. Turn right and go past the Hall of Pentre'r felin, now a large farm. Go over the stile on the left and follow the hedge on your left. Go through the field gate and turn half-right across the field. Go through another gate and follow the hedge on your left to the next field gate. From here go half-right to a stile across this field which will take you onto the Llangwyfan/Llandyrnog road. Turn left and when you see the chapel on your left. Turn right into a little lane which takes you to the car park at the rear of the White Horse Inn.

THE END

INJURING
MILESTONES.

WHEREAS by an Act of Parliament (3d. Geo. 4th. Chapt. 126.) it is enacted that if any Person shall wilfully break, pull up, or damage any Milestone, and be thereof convicted before a Justice of the Peace, such Person so offending, shall forfeit and pay for every such offence, any sum not exceeding

Ten Pounds.

And whereas several of the Milestones on the Turnpike Roads leading from Marchwiel to Whitchurch, and from Redbrook to Welshampton, and from Bangor to Malpas, have of late been broken or otherwise damaged:

IS HEREBY GIVEN,

That all Persons who shall be found so offending in future, will be proceeded against according to law.

BROOKES & LEE,
Clerks to the Trustees of the said Roads.

J. WALFORD, PRINTER, WHITCHURCH.

Turnpike Notice from the Wrexham - Whitchurch Road

114

FOEL-FELEN-YR-YSBYD
(Ghost of the Yellow Mountain)
Dedicated to Peter Jones of Pantymwyn

THE WALK
My eagerness for walking the ancient highways of North Wales has brought surprises in many forms but none like the one which I would witness on this day.

It was a weekend late in November 93 that my friend Peter and I planned a circular walk to investigate part of a holy road and an ancient Packhorse trail which went through the valley of Dolwyddelan and over the hills to the Penmachno. The small community of Dolwyddelan is well known, due to it being close to the famous Roman road, Sarn Helen, which ran between Carmarthen (Moridunum) and Conwy (Kanovium). The medieval holy road that came from the Abbey of Bedd-gelert was reputed to have passed through Dolwyddelan, and along the southern range of hills making its way to Holywell.

We had waited a month for the weather to settle: it had been either raining or too foggy. Finally a clear day arrived: it had snowed the day before and a light frost had settled overnight. The day was crisp with a sharp breeze and the skies were clear.

THE HOLY ROAD

The ford on the River Lledr had been in the vicinity of the road bridge which spanned the river by the Dolwyddelan Railway Station. The station yard was available for vehicle parking and it was well used by other ramblers. Being close to the holy road and the packhorse trail, it was an ideal starting place. We decided to take the easier route first: the holy road and finish with an effortless walk down from the top of the mountains along the packhorse trail.

I had put my thermals on under normal walking gear and a thick woollen jumper, scarf, hat and gloves to keep out the cold from the heavy frost that had settled overnight. Peter, being much younger than me, was more of the hardy type, who never seemed to feel the cold: many a day, when I have been wrapped up, he has been walking with his shirt sleeves rolled up. Our rucksacks were loaded with wet weather gear and lunchtime snacks. Peter always seemed to carry everything but the kitchen sink in his rucksack; he always amazed me at the things that he would pull out of it. With everything ready we set off.

Our route left the car park and along an old quarry road which passed two cottages and a gate that would not open. This track would take us to the remains of the holy road which entered a pass between Foel Felen and the Drosgol Mountains. The start of this old road was like that of an old quarry railway, straight up at first and then onto a short level piece. The next upward stretch was an obstacle course littered with loose stones and small boulders strewn all over the grassy track, causing us to stumble several times: a difficult place to walk in a straight line.

THE QUARRY

The next level section went close to the unfenced high edge of a quarry where a small mountain stream had overflowed sending water cascading into the quarry. This had frozen over making the walk uphill more perilous. Due to my fear of heights and this slippery surface I forced myself through the dead brambles and briars along the opposite edge of the track. It was here that we both spoke at the same time saying that we would not like to travel this old road in the dark. (Little did I know what fate had in store for me later that day.)

116

THE PASS

Tripping over dead branches, falling over hidden boulders, splashing through semi-frozen fords, I was becoming quite wet with perspiration from the effort needed to climb this trail, we slowly made our way into a dark eerie pass between the two mountains. A local tale tells that this pass was haunted by a giant; villagers will not walk through here after dark. Near the upper part of the trail the mountains seem to part, creating a sun soaked hollow, because it was free from the cold winds and the dark gloom. Some of the trees were still in their late summer coats. Even the grass still carried a tinge of pleasant green. It was so warm here it was as if someone had built a large glass cover over the hollow.

The track descends, going back into the real dark gloomy world of winter. A stone wall now lines the right side of the road. Stones and boulders which have fallen from the mountain side above are stopped by this wall, creating rocky obstructions for any traveller. The effort of negotiating these soon began to tell and I was perspiring all the more and I could feel that the legs of my thermals were soaking wet. I began to wish that I had not put them on.

Eventually the trail enters into the Pwll-y-gath valley. Going downhill and around a ruin it meets with the modern lane which runs between the Lledr valley in the north and goes over the hill to our right into the valley of Penmachno. We turned right, and walked uphill to where the lane bends around a rocky outcrop. The holy road leaves the lane on this bend to continue northeast passing by a small riding school. Here several young ladies were busy grooming their mounts in preparation for a ride. After a short delay to catch our breath and a few hello's to the ladies we continued along the holy road. The road along this side of the hill was quite difficult to walk as it went through a small paddock used for the ponies: the surface was pocked with deep hoof prints, and these had frozen hard. From this paddock the trail starts to go downhill going towards the junction of the Lledr valley and the Conwy valley.

IWERDDON MOUNTAIN

Near to Bwlch Maen and leaving the holy road, we turned onto a permissive footpath that would take a route over the mountain to the village of Penmachno. This path is quite steep as it goes uphill through the Iwerddon Forest, a National Trust property. Breaking out of the forest onto the top of mountain moor, flakes of snow floated on the breeze, blowing skilfully, avoiding the clumps of crispy heather that formed a white carpet across the moor. The coolness of the icy breeze froze my wet thermals making it difficult to walk. It was as if I was wearing the legs of a suit of armour when trying to step over these frozen clumps of heather.

117

In the distance there came the sound of screaming car engines, snarling a deep throaty roar, a crash of gnashing gears, then the sound would fade away as the vehicle went along some road in the Penmachno valley below. We thought that some idiots were trying out their cars somewhere in the valley forest below. Reaching the next rows of forest trees and amid the scurrying snow flakes the path had got lost in the snow. If there had been one over this moor then frosty white heather had hidden it. Before the trees there was a high stone wall and splitting up we went either way to find a gap or the path down to the Penmachno village below. At long last Peter shouted, "Here is a gap and something of a path through the trees"

The path ? I think it was probably made by straying sheep. At times we had to crawl on our knees to avoid the over-hanging wooden spears just waiting to penetrate our passing bodies. Eventually after crashing through what seemed a formidable barrier of broken sagging branches and twisting briars, a murky water filled ditch and a large bank, we burst out onto a forest road.

A group of young men standing on this high bank jumped in amazement as we broke through their ranks onto the rugged track, some ran away thinking perhaps that some wild animal had sprang from the forest at them. Recovering from their surprise they hastily re-climbed back to their perch on the top of this slippery grassy bank.

THE RALLY

We stood on the track brushing ourselves down, I tried to wring the mucky waters from the lower legs of my thermals regretting that I had ever put them on. "You had better get off the track," said one of the young men on the bank, " there's another due very soon". Peter and I looked at each other at this. What did he mean another due soon? "What do you mean another one due soon ? " asked Peter. " A car, " was the answer. I repeated, " A car, what car? " expecting some daft answer.

The group of young men as if conducted by some large musicians baton, all shouted at us, " Rally car. You are standing in the way of the RAC Rally. There's another on the way". No sooner had they shouted than there was a distant roar of a deep throated engine, a crash of screaming gears and a cloud of rolling dust appeared at the far end of the track. Peter and I leapt for the bank. I missed and once more entered the murky waters up to my waist. Peter dragged me onto the bank saying something like "Silly old fool," just as the rolling roaring screaming cloud of dust went swirling past.

was in this part of Wales. The excitement of these flying cars soon got to us because we had never been to watch these skilful drivers with fully charged cars in real life, only having seen them on the TV screen from the evening news flashes.

We stood there for some time with cameras out trying to get a glimpse of a car in the swirling dust. What we had not realised was that time was passing quickly, too quickly, and we must move on. This was winter and time mattered. The hour was now high noon and we still had a long way to go to find the Dolwyddelan packhorse trail. With great reluctance we forced ourselves away from the car-mad crowd and across the track onto a descending path, deciding to shorten our journey by trying to find the trail on this hillside above Penmachno.

FAME

We came to another path which turned uphill. We followed this, pushing our way through, crushing people on their way down, crossing more rally tracks, waiting for a whistle to say it was safe to go, it was never ending. Up and up we climbed, stopping, waiting, crossing, until eventually we found the old trail. Peace at last. We both gasped a sigh of relief. At least we were on our way back. Bursting out from overgrown shrubs we were confronted with rows upon rows of caravans, each one advertising what business they were in. T V cables spread across the ground like hidden snakes waiting to trip a passing victim. Out in a clearing and across our path were more rally cars and waiting drivers, T V cameras and the crews, rally officials waving their clipboards.

Deciding to make our way through this thriving throng, a shout went up "Stop ! You can't cross here, go back and go round, " one official was waving his little white board. Pete looked at me and I nodded. By now we were fed up with these so-called officials telling us which way to go. "You can't do this ! You can't do that !" Giving him the famous army salute of two, we barged our way through this car-maddened crowd. "You're on T V," someone shouted as we pushed by. "Good," I shouted out aloud, "fame at last," and continued up the hill along Lledr lane until we were away from the crush.

On reaching the continuation of the packhorse trail we both sank onto a stone, shattered and tired. In our excitement and haste to get away the pangs of hunger were telling us it was time for a snack.

THE RETURN

We sat on that stone for quite a time watching the swirling crowd below, both of us muttering about the rally officials and their flipping little white boards, controlling the swelling crowds as if they were herding sheep across a moor. We talked about our last mad dash; perhaps our folks back home may have seen us go by; to think that my last sign would be seen in thousands of homes across the screen; I'll be famous just like Harvey Smith when he did it on the screen.

Pete nudged me " Come on its time to go, we have two hours of light which should be about right to see us off this trail ". Grudgingly I walked slowly up the track, my legs still wet and very cold from that murky ditch. We had not gone far when a farmer in his Landrover drove down from the trail above, stopping by the side of us and asked if we knew the way over the mountain trail. We admitted that neither of us had ever been here before and we had allowed a two hour walk over the mountain back to Dolwyddelan . He warned us not to go. " The track is dangerous. Even at the height of summer walkers often cannot find the trail and fall into the one of the many bogs that await high on the moor. Besides there is not enough light; its going to be dark within the hour. Go back onto the lane follow it north and down the vale and you will soon be at the holy road, the way you came," he advised.

Agreeing with the farmer, we were both very tired, we decided to make our way back down the lane and holy road. In a way I was glad because I was feeling a bit sickly. Whether it was something that I had eaten or the fumes from the cars, I did not know for certain. Thankfully we would be walking downhill most of the way instead of going up a mountain. It was quite a distance to the medieval road; the little lane twisted and turned around rocky outcrops, making our progress slow downhill. By the time the ruin and the trail came into view the day had turned quite dark and a bright moon began to light the way.

120

Darkness started to fall and a hard frost was setting in. The bottom of my trousers had once again gone stiff, sounding like small clapper boards as the bottom edges met each other as I walked. Turning onto the holy road we felt well rested after the long walk down the hill. "I will go in front, " said Pete as he fetched out a small torch. Walking and stumbling up the trail, the closeness of the mountain pass darkened the passage and moon beams fought their way through the trees as if trying to show the way.

The sickness had left me but now I was starting to feel very giddy and perspiration was breaking out onto my skin which immediately froze. My walk slowed and I started to drop back. Pete kept asking me if I was all right. "Go on I will try keep up," I said, pretending that I had tripped and hurt my foot. I did not want to worry him as to how I really felt. I was stumbling over stones and wishing that we would soon reach the little hollow at the top of the pass. Then the torch dimmed, the batteries were giving out, moon beams still struggled through the trees giving little glimmers of light. At last the hollow was reached. It was so different in the dark. No welcoming light, just a dark ghostly eerie place.

CYCLE TRACKS

With a shiver I remembered about the ghost. I pressed on but by now I could not feel my legs as if a numbness was creeping up above my waist. I must have banged my shins on hidden boulders several times, but I did not feel a thing. I was starting to shiver and my teeth wouldn't stop chattering. I was falling down more times then I was standing up. Pete knew by now that there was something wrong: he couldn't fail to hear my chattering teeth and had seen me go down so many times. Removing his coat and putting it round my shoulders he said, "Not far now, we are on the way down". In the dull light of the torch I spotted cycle wheel marks going off the trail taking another way down, " Lets follow them", I mumbled, " there may be a better way down ".

This trail was on the way down, at last we could see the twinkle of lights of Dolwyddelan village, the sound of cars racing along the main road in the valley below, and the barking of the village dogs as if to herald our coming. Suddenly the cycle marks vanished, stopping at the edge of a very deep quarry. Peter stopped, searched around but could not find which way they had gone down. " We will have to go back up, onto to the trail we know, its not far " he said. By this time I had slumped onto the ground. I couldn't move. The numbness was spreading above my waist. All I wanted to do was to sleep. I felt so tired. I did not want to go back up and I told Pete to leave me here and let me sleep.

Pete is not the type of fellow to panic. He knew that he could not carry me down, not along that slippery stony trail. Pulling off his pack, covering me with his waterproofs, a couple of plastic sheets and my pack under my head, I heard him say, "Stay here, don't go to sleep, I will go and get help try not to sleep, " he emphasised and off he went at a run back to the original trail.

A LIGHT

Don't go to sleep. I could not resist it, snuggling down into a ball under the extra layers. The coldness was spreading through my body and yet I felt quite warm. I could not resist the temptation that was dragging me into a dark dreamy world. I did not care. I just slipped away into that inviting dark warm wilderness. Whether I had slept or how long I dozed I do not know, but something stirred me into consciousness. I opened my eyes. I could not see the village lights which had twinkled through the trees as before. It had gone dark, so dark and inky black on this mountain side.

High in the trees to my side there was a strange yellow glow, flickering as if it was trying to relay some coded message. In the valley below I could see the car headlights speeding along the highway and yet I was puzzled that I could not hear their racing engines or the changing of the gears. There was a deep silence which went right through the valley. Not a dog barked. Not a door clattered. Not a child screamed. The trees were swaying gently and yet I could not hear those rustling leaves. Trying to prop myself up on my elbow I found that I could not move. I was frozen in the solitude of that eerie silence.

Strange thoughts passed through my mind. Have I died ? Am I on the other side ? I found that I could move my fingers but nothing else. I touched my legs; they were like blocks of ice. I tried to force myself to roll but Peter had wedged me so tight that only with great effort I managed to force myself up onto my elbows. I still could not hear a sound in the valley below. My eyes drifted to that yellow flickering glow in the trees.

THE GHOST

Suddenly I was aware that someone was bending over me, picking me up, an arm under my shoulders and one under my legs, heavy breathing, on the strain of lifting some thirteen stone as if I was but a small child. I tried to move to see the face but I was frozen stiff ; all I could see was the pointed brim of a large hat. I tried to speak but my voice did not arrive. I could smell a strong stench of decaying vegetation and mouldy tobacco on something that pushed against the side of my face and yet I could not see the hand of the strong arm under my legs.

Slowly we turned and went up the hill, the strange yellow glow simmered in the darkness on the trees. As I was carried up the hill the glow seemed to move the same way. Then turning again I was carried down the perilous trail. Remembering all the loose stones and boulders that lay on this trail, not once was there a trip or the sound of a footfall as we bore down this slippery slope to the old quarry road below. I was past caring who this person might be, I was still dozy and nothing in me would move, I didn't care, I just lay there like a little child. Then, as if the darkness had lifted, I became aware of the lights of the village coming closer and we were nearing that damned awkward quarry gate. I thought, "Here, who ever it they are, must put me down". Peter and I had found it would not open and had to climb over. But no, I was carried through that gate as if it wasn't there. Passing the little cottages I was slowly coming round, the cold was going and I was starting to feel warmth spreading along my legs. Down the short track and onto the railway yard. I was starting to feel movement in my limbs as I was put down gently by the car.

There was a small street lamp which dimly sent a small passage of light across the station yard. In this low light I could see the outline of a giant of a man. I tried to see the face as he straightened his back. I shivered, for all I could see was a black hollow beneath that hat. He turned and started back. This time I found my voice and called after him, "Who are you? Please stay, I want to thank you", but without a word, without a wave, he carried on up the track.

Passing the little cottages and in the low light I could see a three-cornered hat and a cloak which flowed from around his shoulders. Long wide sleeves adorned his arms and funny type trousers tucked into knee length boots. With great strides he went back the way we had come, and at the closed gate he went straight on as if it was not there, and then he was gone into the deep inky darkness of the hills. The mysterious yellow glow which had been on that mountain side came bright, flickered and then went out.

I struggled for my keys and, as I opened the car door, the sounds of the village drifted back through the darkness: dogs barking, doors clattering, people talking, as if someone had switched it all back on.

RELIEF

In the car boot I had a change of clothes and as I was struggling into these I suddenly remembered Peter: Where was he? I thought that I would wait a few minutes more, as I was starting to feel cold again. I started the engine to get some warmth, then I would try to find him. A few minutes went by and I didn't want to leave all that warmth. My legs had returned to normal except for a tingle in my feet. I lay back in the scat and my thoughts wandered into a sort of a dream of that giant of a man.

Suddenly lights appeared. A vehicle arrived in a squealing of brakes which brought me out of my dream. The vehicle said 'Mountain Rescue' on the side. Seeing me in the car, out jumped Peter and two other men. "How did you get here? I told you to stay where you were. "How did you get here ?" He asked so many questions I could not answer them all at once.

One of the men started to check me over. "Get off," I said, "I'm nice and warm." The man who had looked at me said to his friend "Yes, he's all right, give him the flask". That first cup was the best that I had ever had, it was so sweet. The warmth was flowing through my inside and soon I was starting to feel like myself again. After quite a chat I told my tale. The rescue team said they would have to leave, and with funny looks on their faces, they bade us farewell and drove off the way they had come.

THE PACKS

Peter was still looking in disbelief at how had I managed to get there because when he had left me he said that I was in no fit state. He said finally, "I will have to go back up to get the packs and waterproofs, I can't leave them there all night". I told him to get the other torch from the boot of the car. When he opened the car boot, he sort of stood back in a kind of surprise with his hands up in the air. " What is the matter?" I called and, walking round to the back, I too was amazed to see the two backpacks in the car boot.

Sitting on the back of the car I recalled the previous event but could not remember anything of the backpacks, probably because I was in a sickly state. Peter looked at me in doubt. He said that he did not believe the tale I had told. "Oh heck you must have been out of your head," he muttered with hesitancy, " you somehow brought them down". I pointed out, " How could I carry your pack? You carry everything but the kitchen sink. I could not lift it even when in a fit state".

HISTORICAL FACT

A few months went by and when next in that area I called in to the Mountain Rescue to thank them for their efforts. One of the rangers told me about the local tale which refers to a John Owen in the thirteenth century, a giant amongst men, who was paid by the local lords to patrol the holy road, helping any lost travellers who had strayed from the road. At night, he carried a small oil lamp to hang on a tree to find his way off the moor and back to the road.

Bewick Woodcut

This was not the first time that the rangers had heard of someone having been close to death who had been brought from the mountain to safety by a ghostly giant. He only helps those who are nearing death. I said, " I wasn't close to death. Why did he help me? I had just done too much and a rest had put me back on my feet". The ranger continued, "From the symptoms that your friend described you were in the initial stages of hypothermia. This can strike you down at anytime and if not treated quickly, it will lead to death. If the ghost, giant, mysterious stranger, or whoever you want to call it, had left you there, by the time we had found you, you would have been quite dead!"

THE END

125

OTHER BOOKS AVAILABLE

Gordon Emery 27 Gladstone Road, Chester, CH1 4BZ.
☎ 01244 377955

Miller of Dee The story of Chester Mills and Millers, their Trades and Wares, the Weir, the Water Engine and the Salmon.
Roy Wilding £9.99

Curious Clwyd An album of oddities from Northeast Wales
Gordon Emery £11.95

Curious Clwyd 2
Gordon Emery £11.95

Guide to the Maelor Way
Gordon Emery £6.95

Family Walks on the North Wales Coast
Gordon Emery £5.50

Family Walks in the North Wales Borderlands
Gordon Emery £5.50

Vale of Llangollen
Gordon Emery & John Roberts £4.95

RSPB Guide to Birdwatching in Clwyd £1.50

The Clywedog Trail £2.80

Walks Around Wrexham Maelor: 16 leaflets £4.80

Poems from a small room Chester Poets £5.99

**FAMILY WALKS in Anglesey £5.50   in Snowdonia £5.50
in South Shropshire £5.50 in Mid Wales £5.50**
Please enquire for Family Walks nationwide.

WALKS IN CLWYD Individual guides with directions, map, and illustrations for 99 pence each. Gordon Emery

LLANGOLLEN Horseshoe Falls & Valle Crucis (revised)
LLANGOLLEN Llandyn Hall & Castell Dinas Bran
LLANGOLLEN Pen-y-coed & Pengwern vale
LLANGOLLEN The High Path to Froncysyllte
LLANGOLLEN Llangollen Canal & Trevor Mills
RHYL River Clwyd & Rhuddlan Castle
PRESTATYN Gop Hill & Trelawnyd
CHIRK Castle, Dyke & Canal
CHIRK Aqueduct, Viaduct & Tunnel
GLYNDYFRDWY A Taste of the Berwyns
GLYNDYFRDWY Pen-y-garth
GLYNDYFRDWY Moel Morfydd
DYSERTH Graig Fawr & Bryniau
DYSERTH Cwm & Marion Mills
PANTYMWYN, MOLD The Leete Walk
MARCHWIEL Sontley Moor & Erddig
RUTHIN Old Roads to Ruthin
RUTHIN Llanfair Dyffryn Clwyd (revised)
CAERGWRLE Ditch, Dyke & Castle
PANTYMWYN, MOLD Moel Famau & Cilcain
YSCEIFIOG Ysceifiog Lake
MELIN Y WERN Ffynnon-y-cyff & Halkyn Mountain
DENBIGH Dr Johnson's Haunts
EYTON Three Walks from the Plassey
DENBIGH The Castle & Pont Ystrad
LLANGOLLEN Vivod
WORLD'S END or NEW BRIGHTON A Mountain Trek
ABERGELE The Watchtower & Beyond
ABERGELE Forts & Follies
COLWYN BAY Two Walks from the Bay
HANMER A Welsh Mere & A Holy Well
COEDPOETH Exploring Nant Mill
ACREFAIR Trevor Tower & The Frozen Clock
CEFN-Y-BEDD Cymau & Windy Hill
MELIN Y WERN Bryn Golau & Penycloddiau
LLANDRILLO Craig Uchaf, Head of the Berwyns

Prices subject to change   **Please add £1 P&P on all orders.**

Toll Sign from Tinkersdale Gate in Hawarden
Courtesy of Flintshire Record Office
Photo: Mike Penney